Instructional Units

for Gifted and Talented Learners

Instructional Units

for *Gifted and Talented Learners*

Units

Grades K–6

PRUFROCK PRESS, INC.
P.O. Box 8813
Waco, TX 76714-8813
Phone: (800) 998-2208
Fax: (800) 240-0333
www.prufrock.com

Contents

Dear Educator,

The Texas Association for the Gifted and Talented has a long time commitment to improving instruction for gifted and talented students.

To this end, the Association plans the annual conference, awards certificates to teachers who achieve levels of professional development beyond the minimum required, and recognizes advocates for the gifted: parents, educators, and citizens who care about the success of gifted and talented students. Another Association undertaking has been a continuing effort to provide examples of curriculum rich in effective teaching strategies for educators working with gifted and talented children. This publication is our second endeavor to accomplish this latter goal.

This new offering from TAGT, *Instructional Units for Gifted and Talented Learners, Grades K–6*, contains sample units written, taught, and revised by a group of Texas teachers. The genesis of this new elementary publication came when a group of teachers, primarily from the Dallas area, met for a week-long workshop cooperatively offered by Southern Methodist University and the Texas Association for Gifted and Talented. Materials drafted in that workshop, but untried in the classroom, inspired the Association to invite teachers from around the state to submit successful "tried and true" units for possible inclusion in an elementary curriculum publication. From the group of excellent units which were submitted, the curriculum committee selected 13 for inclusion in the new publication, all of which have been aligned with the recently-approved Texas Essential Knowledge and Skills (TEKS).

To all those who had a part in this important undertaking—participants in the workshop, teachers who submitted units for consideration, and those whose work was finally included—the committee extends its warmest thanks and appreciation. Your leadership in the area of curriculum and instruction for high ability, high potential children is a tribute to your professionalism.

These sample units are yours to adapt and modify to meet the needs of the students in your classrooms. We wish you success as you use them to enrich the learning experiences of your gifted and talented children!

The Curriculum Committee
Ann Wink, Chair
Michael Cannon
Andi Case
Debra Midkiff
Susan Robertson
Laura Young

Unit 1
In Search of Ologies

Areas of Giftedness
- Creativity
- Critical Thinking
- General Intellectual Ability
- Specific Academic Area
  - Science

Grade Levels
K–3

Duration
5 weeks (pullout)

Generalizations
- Every "ology" has its own language.
- "Ologies" are always changing.
- "Ologies" are based on a body of knowledge to which people are continually adding.
- There will always be new "ologies."

Theme:
Discovery

Grade Levels:
K–3

Developers:
Mary Dyer
Oscar Figueroa
Mary Morris
Becky Newsom
Shannon O'Brien
Sue Renfro

Objective	Activities	Interdisciplinary Connections
• Students will demonstrate risk-taking skills through support of their own ideas while discovering individual differences. See Lesson Plan 1, Page 4	• **Brainstorm a list of living things. Discuss the difference between living and non-living things.** • **KWL chart on biology. Begin biology chart. Add the branch of the day (humans/people).**	• Science • Language Arts
• Students will determine points of views, ideas, and attributes by using partial visual illustrations following oral directions. See Lesson Plan 2, Page 6	• **Play animal trivia in teams. Investigate a variety of resources.** • **Analyze and categorize attributes.** • **Small-group research from animal books.** • **Triangle-ope activity: The students draw an unusual animal described by the teacher.** • **Animal abstractions: Small groups or pairs will decide and record what animal each picture looks like.**	• Science, Language Arts • Science • Creativity, Visual Arts, Language Arts
• Students will use divergent thinking to generate many ideas and possible solutions. • Students will use convergent thinking to integrate those ideas and produce an answer based on given information. See Lesson Plan 3, Page 6	• **Small groups research/explore books and magazines to examine fish and shark attributes. List unusual and interesting facts.** • **Web *Ichthyology* in a large group: Discuss and categorize. Include such categories as body style, environment, sharks, types of fish, etc.** • **Introduce divergent and convergent thinking using the funnel poster. Discuss the meaning of both types of thinking. Share examples.** • **Kriss Kross Grid (divergent) thinking. Brainstorm ideas that apply in each category.** • **Read the Dudley Detective Story.** • **Mystery Creatures Story and Pictures. Solve the mystery.** • **Extensions. Choose an Ichthyology word maker. Make as many words as you can out of fish words.**	• Science • Language Arts

Authentic Methods and Context	Resources	Assessment
	• Hechtman, J.M., Mester, T., & Grove, S.F. (1994). *I'm glad I'm me: Self-esteem for young learners*. Creative Teaching Press.	• Anecdotal notes, student observation.
• Students have the opportunity to interview professionals who work in zoos about the animals they study.	• Goaman, K., & Amery, H. (1984). *Mysteries and marvels of the animal world*. EDC Publications.	• Class-created list of mammal characteristics.
	• Rasmussen, G. (1990). *Play by the rules*. Stanwood, WA: Tin Man Press.	• Compare and contrast.
	• Rasmussen, G. (1984). *The great unbored bulletin board book*. Stanwood, WA: Tin Man Press.	• Compare answers and thinking to answers in book.
• Invite experts in the area of oceanography to help students understand the contribution that the creatures of the ocean make to our world, (i.e., products and their uses).		• Fluency of ideas, anecdotal records.
		• Results of activities will be recorded noting original ideas and extraordinary fluency.
	• Nichols, J., Thomson, S., Wolfe, M., & Merritt, D. (1997). *Primary education thinking skills*. Marion, IL: Pieces of Learning.	• Mystery creature accuracy.

Objective	Activities	Interdisciplinary Connections
• Students will demonstrate their understanding of the creative thinking model Fluency Flexibility Originality Elaboration (FFOE). See Lesson Plan 4, Page 7	• **Share and discuss Cetology materials.** • **Brainstorm things that are enormous.** • **Flexibility—categorize items on fluency list.** • **Small groups create poster or creation of most original "enormous" idea.** • **Elaboration—enhance posters or creation.**	• Science • Language Arts
• Students will compare and contrast attributes to classify a variety of different objects and support their thinking. See Lesson Plan 5, Page 8	• **Brainstorm attributes of a shell. Discuss characteristics. Investigate a variety of resources.** • **Introduce attributes of Malacology. Shell collections should be brought from home by students.** • **Classify shells on Venn poster. Discuss characteristics and support classifications.** • **Classify pictures on Venn poster. Each student will cut and glue pictures onto a Venn.**	• Language Arts, Science • Language Arts, Science • Language Arts, Science • Language Arts, Science, Social Studies

Lesson Plan 1

In Search of Ologies
Biology

Lesson Objectives

Students will demonstrate risk-taking skills through support of one's own ideas.

Prerequisite Skills

Perceiving—this is the first lesson of the year. It is designed to help you get to know the students.

Materials

"Ology" Explorations Poster, brown, green, and white construction paper for Biology tree, Brainstorming poster, lunch sacks for Me Bag.

Introduction

Boundary Breaker: How did you feel when you were on your way to class today?

Introduce the word of the week: *Biology*–the study of all living things.

Activity Descriptions

Have magazines out that the students will look through to explore different ologies. (i.e., *World, Ranger Rick, Zoobook, Eyewitness*.)

1. Biology tree activity. Students make a tree from brown and green construction paper mounted on white. Students write the names of their five favorite living things.
2. Introduce the brainstorming poster. Talk about what brainstorming means. Review and discuss rules. Brain-storm a list of living things.

Authentic Methods and Context	Resources	Assessment
	• Nichols, J., Thomson, S., Wolfe, M., & Merritt, D. (1997). *Primary education thinking skills*. Marion, IL: Pieces of Learning.	• Teacher observation.
• Students will research the effects of ecology on quality of shells. Invite an environmentalist to speak.		• Diagnostic notes for scoring fluency, flexibility.
		• Anecdotal records. Evaluate student participation. Teacher observation.
		• Evaluate student participation in whole and small-group activities.
		• Discuss and evaluate each student's work and the thinking behind his or her decision, based on pre-established criteria.

3. Introduce word of the week: Biology. Define: Study of living things. As part of our "ology" study this year, we will have a word that we will study each week.

4. Show map on branches of Biology. Today we will concentrate on one branch of biology. Add new branches to a chart each week.

5. KWL chart on Biology. K = What you <u>know</u> already. W = what you <u>want</u> to know. L = What you <u>learned</u>.

6. Reflection log: Write anything new that students learned.

Closure

Take a few seconds and think of the new things you have learned today. (Give children time to think.) Have children share with a neighbor or class. Connect activities and thinking to the four content areas.

Extensions

With your family, brainstorm a list of hobbies, possessions, and favorite things. Choose three items from your list that best represents you. Bring those things to class in your "Me Bag" next week.

Assessment
• Anecdotal notes.
• Student observations.

Lesson Plan 2

In Search of Ologies
Zoology

Lesson Objectives

The student will determine different points of view, ideas, and attitudes.

Prerequisite Skills

Brainstorming, Application Attributes, Teamwork, Observing, and Analysis.

Materials

Animal books, *Play by The Rules,* "The Triangle-ope," Page 66.

Introduction

Boundary Breaker: Name an animal that is the most like you and tell why.

Introduce word of the week: *Zoology*—the study of the animal kingdom.

Activity Descriptions

1. The teacher asks the class animal trivia questions about mammals. In teams, children try to guess the names of the animals as a fun way to learn facts about mammals. The teacher lists the names of the animals on the board. Analyze and categorize attributes of these animals to come up with these four characteristics of mammals.

   - Mammals nurse their young.
   - Mammals have hair.
   - Mammals bear their young alive.
   - Mammals are vertebrates (they have a backbone).

2. In small groups, the children will use books and magazines for 15 minutes to research animals. They will share with the class interesting facts that they discovered.

3. Creative Cultivation Activity—"The Triangle-ope." The children listen as the teacher describes an unusual animal. They will draw a picture of it in their individual logs. After completing the activity, the children will compare and contrast their drawings and discuss how individuals picture or perceive ideas differently. Then, the teacher will show the picture from the book.

4. Animal abstractions: In a small group or as a whole, the children look at the animal abstraction page. They will decide what animal each picture looks like and record their answers. This activity will provide for a great discussion and children can share their reasoning for their answers. They will determine different points of view and the related effects on ideas and attitudes. The whole class will meet afterward and compare their answers to the ones given in the book.

Closure

Students will write or draw their ideas about Zoology in their individual logs. They will share and discuss.

Extensions

Students may create a new animal by combining two of their favorites. They will draw their new animal and write about it. Students could write a dialogue between an animal and its keeper.

Assessment

Teacher observation of teamwork and decision making. Record.

Lesson Plan 3

In Search of Ologies
Ichthyology

Lesson Objectives

Students will use divergent thinking to generate many ideas and possible solutions. Students will use convergent thinking to integrate those ideas and produce an answer based on given information.

Prerequisite Skills

Brainstorming and Categorizing

Materials

Funnel, fish books, magazines, and *Primary Education Thinking Skills.*

Activity Descriptions

1. In small groups, the children will use books and magazines to do 15 minutes of research on fish attributes.
2. In a large group, web the word Ichthyology on a large chart.
3. Kriss Kross Grid—divergent thinking (one per pair or group of children; see Attachment 1, page 9): Categories are dangerous things, water things, salty things, things that float, large things, and hairy things. The letters across the top are FISH. The children will have their own page, but can work in pairs.
4. Read the "Dudley the Detective" story from *Primary Education Thinking Skills.* With students, review these points from the story.
   - In deductive thinking, there is only one right answer. All students should arrive at the same answer to be considered correct.
   - The students may feel like saying, "Aha!" or "I have it!" when they find the right answers.
   - It is often necessary to put more than one clue together in order to find the needed information to solve the problem.
   - Patience is important. Avoid jumping to conclusions or relying on preconceived notions.
5. Have the children listen to the "Mystery Creatures" story from *Primary Education Thinking Skills* and draw the real creatures.

Closure

Name a type of thinking we've studied today and tell us what you've learned about it. Share a time when you used divergent or convergent thinking in your classroom. Describe the other kind of thinking and how you use it. What is this type of thinking called? Can you tell us about a time you've used divergent or convergent thinking?

Have students discuss the subjects they study at school. When is convergent thinking used? Divergent? As you've thought about divergent and convergent thinking, which type of thinking seems to be used more in your classroom? Give an example of a divergent question and a convergent question.

Extensions

Rearrange the letters in Ichthyology to see how many words you can make. Choose another "fishy" word and try again.

Assessment

Score grid for fluency, flexibility, and originality. Design a rubric.

Lesson Plan 4

In Search of Ologies
Cetology

Lesson Objectives

Students will demonstrate their understanding of the creative thinking model Fluency, Flexibility, Originality, and Elaboration (FFOE) by creating original products.

Prerequisites

Brainstorming, Compare/Contrast, and Observation

Materials

Whale echo tape, FFOE poster, whale books and magazines, unique ideas worksheet.

Introduction

Discuss Cetology—the study of whales. Share posters, books, magazines, and materials with the class. Divide the class into three groups.

Teacher says, "Hello," and each group repeats in sequence (to simulate echo) "Where are you?" "It's dark," and "I'm scared." What does this activity remind you of? What did you hear (echo)? Discuss *echolocation* at this time. Echolocation is a way of finding something by carefully listening to its echo. Today we will be using our creative FFOE thinking model and our knowledge of whales to be creative thinkers.

Activity Descriptions
1. Brainstorm a list of things that are enormous. Use the FFOE poster and discuss how *fluency* means many ideas. Count the number of ideas.
2. Discuss the meaning of *flexibility* (many categories of ideas). Discuss which ideas can go together and label the categories. Add new categories that the students didn't list.
3. Discuss the meaning of *originality* (most unusual idea). In small groups, the students will use the fluency list to discuss the idea they feel is most original. The group can make a small poster on white construction paper to show the class their unusual, enormous idea.
4. Discuss the meaning of *elaboration* (adding details). With the class, discuss how elaboration enhances a picture and adds to its originality. Let the small groups discuss what else they could add to make their pictures better.

Closure
How could you use originality and elaboration when you dress for school? How do your parents use these skills at work and home? Think of other times when you can use FFOE. Give examples. How can learning about whales help you or your thinking?

Extensions
Design a device to prevent a whale from beaching.

Assessment
Teacher Observation. Diagnostic notes, *Primary Education Thinking Skills* (Nichols, Thomson, Wolfe, & Merritt, p. 70).

Lesson Plan 5

In Search of Ologies
Malacology/Deductive Thinking

Lesson Objectives
Students will compare and contrast attributes to classify a variety of different objects and support their thinking.

Prerequisite Skills
Observing attributes.

Materials
Large shell, *Encarta*, shell books, magazines, and collections, 3-circle Venn poster, dictionary, Venn worksheet, Attachment 2 (page 10), discovery log,

Introduction
Have students sit on the floor in a circle.

"This summer on our vacation, I found a special item. This is it." Hold up the shell.

"You may examine it more closely as we pass it around the circle. When it is your turn to hold it, please share an attribute of it with the class."

At the end of the activity, say, "From what you have just heard, what is an attribute?"

Activity Descriptions
Today you are going to become *Malacologists*. Can you figure out what "ology" we are going to study today? Does your homework give you a clue? Yes, we will look at shells, but do you know where they come from? *Malacology* is not just the study of shells, it is also the study and science of the soft-bodied creatures that make shells. They are called *mollusks*.

1. Introduce attributes of Malacology. See Mollusk Key (Attachment 2, page 10). In small groups, students will investigate a variety of resources that have been brought from home or provided by the teacher. They may take notes, draw pictures, and so forth, in their discovery log. Students will return to the whole group to share and compare information they have gathered.
2. Have students choose their favorite shell that they brought from home. Show and discuss the 3-circle Venn poster.

Attachment 1

Categories	F	I	S	H
Dangerous				
Water Things				
Salty Things				
Things That Float				
Large Things				
Hairy Things				

Smooth　　**Small**

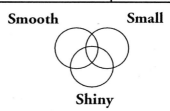

Shiny

Flyers　　**Mammals**

Hard Coverings

Cetology, Ichthyology, Malacology. Students choose three "ologies" to prepare an individual 3-circle Venn.

Stress the importance and attributes of each intersection. As the students sit in a circle on the floor, they will examine their own shell and decide which attributes are characteristics of it. Then, each student will place their shell on the Venn and explain their decision.

3. Independent activity: have students cut out magazine pictures and paste each picture on a section of the 3-circle Venn worksheet.

When complete, compare and give an explanation of each picture placement.

Closure

- What did we do with shells today?
- What is an attribute?
- What thinking skill did we use (classification)?
- How does understanding attributes help us do classification?
- Can you restate the use of the intersections? Why is it helpful?
- List "ologies" studied to date: Biology, Zoology,

Extensions

When you look at shells from now on, what might you focus on? Do you have any new information that you thought was interesting? Do you use classification in school? At home? Compare learning with generalizations. What are the core content connections for today's lesson?

This could be a stopping point for this unit, although the class could study "ologies" all year.

Assessment

Independent Venn activity.

Attachment 2

Mollusk Key

Any one of a large group of animals that:

- have no backbone;
- have soft bodies not composed of segments;
- are usually covered with a hard shell of one or more parts; and
- have a shell that is secreted by a covering mantle and is formed on snails, clams, oysters, whelks, and mussel.

Slugs, octopi, and squids have no shells. Mollusks make up a family in the animal kingdom.

Unit 2
Unwrapping the Gifts

Areas of Giftedness
- Creative Thinking
- General Intellectual Ability
- Leadership
- Science
- Specific Academic Area
  - Fine Arts

Grade Levels
K–3

Duration
8–10 weeks

Generalizations
- Relationships exist between giftedness, affective issues and achievement.
- Exploring relationships of great/gifted people promotes self-growth.
- Investigating attributes common to the areas of giftedness promotes self-awareness and success as well as reflecting student understanding of giftedness.
- Research assists individuals in gaining insight into the life of a gifted person.

Theme:
Relationships

Grade Levels:
K–3

Developer:
Susan Robertson

Objective	Activities	Interdisciplinary Connections
• While investigating the lives of great people, the students will explore relationships among gifted people.	• Engage in a game of "Who Am I?" Use names of gifted people who are familiar to the students (e.g., U.S. President, principal, teacher, athlete, actor, etc.). • Complete a pre-assessment of personal awareness of giftedness and analyze responses through a group discussion (e.g., What do you think being gifted means? How should a gifted person feel or act? Should he or she be treated differently?).	• Social Studies, Language Arts
• In their study of the five areas of giftedness, the students will explore attributes common to those areas.	• Experience characteristics of each area of giftedness by participating in fast-paced activities (e.g., "Simon Says" = leadership, trivia questioning = general intellectual). • Introduce areas of giftedness using symbols and brainstorm what area they represent (e.g., leadership = gavel or teacher = bell).	
	• Complete student assessment of gifts/strengths. Create a "Collage of Myself" to display individual gifts. • Brainstorm personal characteristics that have been found to contribute to achievement and success. • Explain and demonstrate importance of divergent thinking. • Incorporate risk-taking activities that parallel experiences of gifted people. • Create a group cheer promoting success. • Display the quote, "The human mind is like an umbrella. It functions best when open." Interpret the analogy. • Create other analogies that compare the human mind to something different.	
	• Role play an interview with a gifted student. • Review district identification process. In small groups assume the role of a screening committee for a gifted program. • Evaluate student profiles for famous people whose names have been changed. Class comes to a consensus as to which student should be placed in a gifted program. Teacher reveals true identities. • Read and discuss *Albert Einstein*. • Relate the fact that everyone makes mistakes or has had an embarrassing moment and learned from them. • Read excerpts from *Live and Learn and Pass It On*. Students create an original phrase (e.g., "I've learned ...").	• Social Studies

Authentic Methods and Context	Resources	Assessment
	• Gudeman, J. (1996). *Creative encounters with creative people.* School Specialty Children's Publishing.	• Class discussions with teacher observation.
	• Gudeman, J. (1996). *Learning from the lives of amazing people.* School Specialty Children's Publishing.	
	• Balsamo, K. (1987). *Exploring the lives of gifted people in the sciences.* School Specialty Children's Publishing.	
• Invite a community resource person from any or all areas to speak to students about gifts, talents, struggles, and achievements.	• Balsamo, K. (1987). *Exploring the lives of gifted people in the arts.* School Specialty Children's Publishing.	
• Interview members of the district's selection committee.	• District's Identification policy.	• Group discussion with teacher observations.
• After a visit by a school counselor or a community counselor in which they share strategies for dealing with teasing, students will role play a counseling situation between counselor and gifted student.	• Lepscky, I. (1992). *Albert Einstein.* Barron's Educational Series, Inc. • Brown, H.J. (2000). *Live and learn and pass it on: Volumes I & II.* Thomas Nelson.	

Objective	Activities	Interdisciplinary Connections
See Lesson Plan 1, Page 16	• Conduct a CoRT PMI on perfectionism. • Play the questioning game, "What's in the Box?" using a band-aid. Predict what the band-aid may symbolize. • Share the myth of Achilles. Discuss the term *Achilles' Heel*. • Introduce *Self Talk* posters. Create a personal self talk poster. Encourage daily self talk. • Read *Tacky the Penguin* or sing *Rudolph the Red-Nosed Reindeer*. Discuss the dilemma. • Stressing fluency, brainstorm names, nicknames, and/or phrases a gifted kid could be called and reasons why he or she might be made fun of. Role play teasing situations. • Decorate a "gift box" reflecting individual's personality traits. Fill with items that symbolize unique gifts.	
• In their investigation of great/gifted students will share knowledge through an oral, written, or visual presentation. See Lesson Plan 2, Page 16	• Review strategies for divergent and convergent thinking. Students complete a di-con. • Read a biography and research a gifted person's life. • Create a personality box, coat of arms, character cube, or other product depicting the personality traits and areas of giftedness.	• Language Arts
• The students will use what they have learned about the areas of giftedness to author a book that reflects their understanding of giftedness.	• Read, interpret, and discuss Nathan Levy's *There Are Those*. • Author an original book about being gifted. This could be an autobiography, biography, fictional story dealing with gifted issues, a book of poems, or interviews of gifted friends.	

Authentic Methods and Context	Resources	Assessment
	• DeBono, E. (1986). *CoRT thinking skills.* Easterville, OH: SRA.	
	• Addirholdt-Elliot, M. (1989). *Perfectionism: What's so bad about being good?.* Minneapolis, MN: Free Spirit.	
	• Delisle, J. (1987). *Gifted kids speak out.* Minneapolis, MN: Free Spirit.	
	• Dale Bulla's *Self Talk* inspirational posters.	
• Visit a high school humanities class. Students act as investigative reporters interviewing high school students about the challenges of growing up gifted. Videotape if possible.	• Bianch, J. (1988). *Tacky the penguin.* Boston, MA: Houghton Mifflin.	
• Humanities students become mentors to help students understand their giftedness.		
• Students assume the role of a famous gifted person they have researched and participate in a simulated talk show called *Star Chat.* Teacher assumes role as emcee.		• Teacher, student, and peer evaluations will be used in a rubric that incorporates instructor and student chosen criteria.
	• Levy, N., & Levy, J. (1994). *There are those.* NL Association.	
	• Product Guide Kits by The Curriculum Project, Inc.	

Lesson Plan 1

Unwrapping the Gifts
Understanding Giftedness

Lesson Objectives

In their study of the five areas of giftedness, students will explore attributes common to these areas.

Prerequisite Skills

Understanding there are five areas of giftedness. Each person is unique, not all are gifted in the same way.

Materials

Box, band-aids, art supplies, Dale Bulla's *Self Talk* poster.

Introduction

Brainstorm things you are really good at and things that are hard for you or do not come naturally or easy.

Activity Descriptions

1. Play the questioning game, "What's in the Box?"
2. Share the myth of Achilles. Discuss: Would you like to be invulnerable? What do you think the term *Achilles' Heel* means? The myth helps us realize that everyone has weaknesses (is vulnerable). Could an Achilles' heel be a weakness besides a spot on your body?
3. Brainstorm human weaknesses.
4. Analyze a personal Achilles' heel and identify a band-aid or a way to overcome this weakness. Students choose a variety of ways that the band-aid could be shared with the class (advertisement, cartoon, poem, skit, etc.).
5. Introduce Dale Bulla's *Self Talk* posters. Create a personal self talk poster using various art supplies. Display poster in the room or school hallway to encourage campus self talk.

Closure

Students share, discuss, and evaluate products. Daily self talk is encouraged.

Extensions

Students may create family self talk posters that would encourage and strengthen the family members. Record Achilles' heel (weakness) in journal and create a plan of action to overcome weakness and reach chosen goals.

Assessment

Teacher, student, and peer-evaluations that incorporate instructor and student chosen criteria will be used as well as attributes of products from the Product Guides.

Lesson Plan 2

Unwrapping the Gifts
Giftedness

Lesson Objectives

In their study of the five areas of giftedness, the students will explore attributes common to these areas.

Prerequisite Skills

Understanding there are five areas of giftedness and each person is unique and not all are gifted in the same way.

Materials

Overhead projector

Introduction

Review Bloom's *Taxonomy of Thinking*.

Activity Descriptions

1. Review the application level of thinking by asking students to paraphrase its definition.
2. Review strategies of effective gifted people by describing the difference between divergent and convergent thinking.
3. Introduce di-con list by modeling a sample list on the overhead.
   a. Place keyword *risk taking* at the top of the list.
   b. For two minutes do divergent thinking, listing the next word that

comes to mind by free association.

c. At the end of the two minutes, draw a line under the last word recorded.

d. In as few words as possible, do convergent thinking relating the last word back to the first word.

e. Justify response.

Example: risk taking
>
> brave
> explorers
> heroes
> strong
> weak
> day
> sun
> moon
> <u>stars</u>
> heroes
> explorers
> risk takers

Closure

Students share di-cons by elaborating on their thinking and connections between the first word and the word where the line was drawn.

Extensions

Students may write a poem or story using words from the di-con list.

Assessment

Completed list will be evaluated by teacher-developed rating scale to include the creative and critical thinking process.

Notes

Unit 3
Over the Rainbow

Areas of Giftedness
- Creative Thinking
- General Intellectual Ability
- Leadership
- Science
- Specific Academic Area
  - Fine Arts

Grade Levels
2-3

Duration
14 weeks (Pullout)
7 weeks (Cluster)

Generalizations
- Exploring light and color relationships promote understanding.
- Connections exist between color and mood.
- Exploring various art forms broadens awareness of ourselves and others.
- Exploring relationships between types of art promotes appreciation of cultural and aesthetic venues.

**Theme:
Exploring
Relationships in
Light, Color,
and Art**

**Grade Levels:
2-3**

**Developer:
Laura Young**

Objective	Activities	Interdisciplinary Connections
• In their study of color and light, students will conduct various experiments related to color and record their findings.	• **Discover the origin of color by discussing "Where does color come from?" Research the life of Sir Isaac Newton.**	• Science, Language Arts, Art
	• **Discover that light is bent or refracted to cause a spectrum by shining a light beam through a prism.**	• Science
	• **Investigate the electromagnetic spectrum and term *Roy G. Biv* (red, orange, yellow, green, blue, indigo, violet).**	• Science
	• **Discover how a rainbow is formed by placing a clear glass of water in the light of an overhead. The projector is like the sun and the water is like moisture in the air. When the room is darkened and the light beam shines through the glass, a spectrum will appear.**	• Science
	• **Deduce that the combination of all colors in light make white light by covering three flashlights with a different color of cellophane on each: red, green, and blue. Shine all of the colors on the same spot.**	• Science
	• **Research the role that the eyes and brain play in our ability to see color.**	
See Lesson Plan 1, Page 26	• **Explore the concept of after-image by demonstrating how eye nerves can tire of colors and seem to see colors that are not there. (See Attachment 1, page 28.)**	• Science
• By using research and investigative skills, students will determine how color affects the many areas of our daily lives.	• **Utilize a photometer (see Attachment 2, page 29) to discover that colors do not exist without light and that the color of an object is really the color of the light it reflects. Summarize results in a paragraph.**	• Science, Language Arts
	• **Brainstorm a list of feelings, characteristics, and attributes associated with each color. Have them write an analogy comparing themselves to their favorite color.**	• Language Arts
	• **Create a diamante, cinquain, haiku, or acrostic poem about a favorite color.**	• Language Arts
	• **Evaluate the concept of a world without color. List the pluses and minuses on a chart.**	• Science, Language Arts

Authentic Methods and Context	Resources	Assessment

Authentic Methods and Context	Resources	Assessment
	• Catherall, E. (1989). *Exploring lights.* Austin, TX: Steck-Vaughn Library.	
	• Walpole, B. (1987). *Light.* New York: Warwick Press.	
	• *Colors.* New York: Scholastic.	
	• Whyman, K. (1989). *Rainbows to lasers.* Gloucester Press.	
	• National Geographic (Producer). (n.d.). *Color: Light fantastic* [Motion Picture].	
	• *World Book Encyclopedia,* "Color."	• Orally share findings with the class.
	• Encyclopedias.	
	• *Groiler* CD-ROM.	
	• Wayman, J. (1988). *Colors of my rainbow.* Pieces of Learning.	• Teacher-selected criteria will be used to evaluate paragraph.
	• O'Neill, M. (1989). *Hailstones and halibut bones: Adventures in color.* New York: Doubleday.	• Graphs and student activity will be evaluated by a rubric that incorporates instructor and student chosen criteria.
	• DeBono, E. (1986). *CoRT thinking skills.* Easterville, OH: SRA.	• Teacher and peer-devised rubric will be used to evaluate advertisements.

21

Objective	Activities	Interdisciplinary Connections
See Lesson Plan 2, Page 26	• **Hypothesize how color affects choices. Determine color preference by surveying a population (Attachment 3, page 29). Categorize information accumulated on a graph and record in a lab journal.**	• Science, Math, Language Arts
	• **Collect samples from magazine or paper scraps to create a color collage showing the varied shades and hues one color can have.**	• Science
	• **Groups work together as "color scientists" to create a color that hasn't been invented or developed yet. Design an advertisement to "sell" it to the public.**	• Science
	• **Design and construct a unique kaleidoscope using student-selected creative materials. Design a "colorful pursuit" game (like *Trivial Pursuit*) with categories being different colors and answers having color words in them (Attachment 4, page 30).**	• Science, Language Arts • Language Arts, Science, Math
	• **Compare an uncommon color to something else (synectics). For example: "Scarlet is like a volcano blowing itself apart."**	• Science
	• **Compose a unique logic problem relating to color and mood. Compile a class book of logic grids to use as a center or as brainteasers.**	• Science
	• **Organize colors into two families: warm colors (reds, oranges, yellows) and cool colors (blues, purples, greens). Draw two pictures of the same thing. Use cool colors on one and warm on the other. Analyze the differences between the types of colors and mood responses.**	• Language Arts
• In their exploration into different types art, students will research art forms and create original products to demonstrate their understanding.	• **Determine the subjects for paintings (people, objects, scenery) and classify sample pictures.**	• Art, Social Studies
	• **Compare and contrast different artistic styles in paintings (realistic, abstract) using sample pictures.**	• Art, Social Studies
	• **Research labels that artists can be classified as: expressionist, abstract, social realist, cubist, pop-art and op-art (Attachment 5, page 30).**	• Language Arts, Arts

Authentic Methods and Context	Resources	Assessment
		• Visual display and presentation will be evaluated by a rubric that incorporates teacher and student-chosen criteria.
	• Mayer, S., & Reese, B.D. (1981). *American images.* International Myopi.	
• Explore artistic labels and style by participating in art demonstrations by local artists. Students work with artists to create original work.	• Local artists as guest speakers.	• Teacher and student-designed evaluation scale for individual displays.

Objective	Activities	Interdisciplinary Connections
	• Explore various artistic media. Create a masterpiece using a medium of choice. Classify into one of the categories from Attachment 6.	• Art
	• Devise a center activity for classmates to discover each type of art by giving examples of artists that fit into the category (Attachment 6, page 31).	• Language Arts, Art, Social Studies
	• Students experiment with various art forms to create samples for a personal portfolio.	• Art
	• Examine photography as an art form.	• Art
	• Design and photograph an "I Spy" layout.	• Science, Art
	• Research camouflage, mimicry, and counter-shading to decide how color helps animals.	• Science, Art
• In their study of art, students will research gifted artists and share knowledge through an oral, written, or visual presentation.	• Conclude how an artist's feelings influence his or her work. Research the lives of artists. Devise a visual display and an oral presentation to convey findings. For example, wax museum: students become a wax figure of an artist preparing 2–3 minute speech. Viewers activate artists at their leisure.	• Social Studies, Art
	• Research the age when famous artists began painting and sold their first work. Plot on a chart to determine the average age. Draw conclusions based on discovered information (include Alexandra Nechita, the 12-year-old Russian "Picasso").	• Language Arts, Social Studies, Art
	• Interpret information about Vincent Van Gogh and deduce how his life experiences influenced his art.	• Language Arts, Art
	• Create a class art museum to display masterpieces of classroom artists. Students may have individual showings or display one type of art with the help of classmates.	• Language Arts, Art

Authentic Methods and Context	Resources	Assessment
	• Wick, W., & Marzollo, J. (1992). *I spy, a book of picture riddles.* New York: Scholastic Books. • Encyclopedias. • Cummings, P. (1992). *Talking with artists.* New York: Bradbury Press. • *Artists for children* series, E. Roboff. • Microsoft Art Gallery CD-ROM.	• Visual display and presentation will be evaluated by a rubric that incorporates teacher and student-chosen criteria.
	• www.google.com • Thomas, K. (1996, June 27). Alexandra Nechita may be a budding Picasso. *USA Today*, p. D1.	
• Experience the works of artists by visiting an art museum. Work with a local art gallery to be student docents for showing of personal works created throughout the unit.	• McLean, D. (2003). Vincent (Starry Starry Night). On *American pie: Original recording remastered* [CD]. Hollywood, CA: Capitol. • Artwork: "The Starry Night" by Van Gogh. • Luchner, L. (1987). *Vincent Van Gogh.* Scroll Press, Inc.	• Teacher and student-designed evaluation scale for displays.

Lesson Plan 1

Over the Rainbow
Colors

Lesson Objectives

By utilizing research and investigative skills, students will determine how color effects daily life choices.

Prerequisite Skills

Origin of color and color effects of mood.

Materials

Large bags of M&M's (non-seasonal colors).

Introduction

Notice the colors of clothes worn by individual students and colors of cars in the parking lot. Discuss color choices and reasons why some might choose particular colors.

Activity Descriptions

1. Discuss how color is used in art, science, and advertising.
2. Hypothesize how color affects choices. Ask students if they think color makes a difference in choosing food.
3. Predict whether or not color will affect candy preference. Show candies and explain that they all taste the same, but are different colors.
4. In small groups, students do descriptive research by asking a random sampling of people to pick an M&M off a tray containing many M&M's.
5. Students return to class to tally and graph their results. Discuss findings.
6. Each group shares their results with the class.
7. Categorize the class results on a graph or other visual representation.

Closure

Students share, discuss, and evaluate hypothesis. Eat the leftovers!

Extensions

1. Students may survey the entire school and categorize the results by age/grade to see if that makes a difference. Students may wish to announce the results to the entire school.
2. Write a letter to a candy company explaining the results.
3. Conduct "undercover" research by observing a staff member's clothing preferences for two weeks. Do the color choices reflect the person's personality or mood?

Assessment

Completed graphs and oral activity summarization reports will be evaluated by the teacher.

Lesson Plan 2

Over the Rainbow
Colors

Lesson Objectives

In their study of color and light, students will conduct various experiments related to color and record their findings.

Prerequisite Skills

Knowledge of how the eyes and brain see color.

Materials

Kit made of: one sheet of white paper, colored construction paper (4 x 5)—one color for each color on the spectrum, (See Attachment 1, page 20).

Introduction

Flash a camera in the classroom and ask the students to describe what they see and how they feel. Explain: just as the eye nerves respond to the flash, they also respond to the colors we see.

Activity Descriptions

1. Review how we see color. Remind students that the brain organizes nerve signals from the eye and interprets them as colored visual images.
2. Tell students: Many operations of the eyes and brain work automatically and almost instantly in providing us with color vision.

3. Introduce discussion of color vision effects.

4. Hand out previously prepared after-image kit. Have students pick one of the colored pieces of paper and stare at it for 45 seconds.

5. Students should stop staring at the paper, then look quickly at the white paper. On Attachment 1 (page 28), have students record the color they see. Do this for each of the colors. Stress that students need to concentrate on only one color at a time for this to work. Following each image, have students record their findings.

6. After all of the colors are seen, discuss the findings. Ideally, the after-image of each color will be the complimentary color (red/green, blue/orange, yellow/violet). Discuss that the picture seen after closing the eyes or looking away is called an after-image. Nerve endings see each other, get tired, and stop responding.

Closure

Discuss individual findings and summarize the experience in lab journals.

Extensions

1. View example of after-image art work (example: the after-image flag in *World Book* Encyclopedia).

Students design their own after-image picture.

2. Explore phantom colors, color vision in animals, and color blindness in humans.

Assessment

The summarized experience will be evaluated by teacher observation.

Attachment 1
After-Image Documentation Sheet

Color Viewed	After-Image
Red	
Orange	
Yellow	
Green	
Blue	
Purple	

What are your impressions or observations about this activity?

_____
_____
_____
_____
_____
_____

Attachment 2
Photometers

Look at a red apple or another object. The orange, yellow, blue, green, indigo, and violet light are absorbed and only red is reflected back to you. Demonstrate this concept by using a photometer. Students can make their own photometers. They will need two blocks of household paraffin of the same size and shapes; a sheet of aluminum foil about twice the size of the blocks, and two rubber bands. Fold the aluminum foil in half, shiny side out. Place foil between the blocks of wax and secure the blocks with a rubber band at each end. The foil prevents light from going from one block to the other. The photometer can be used to compare the brilliance of two light sources, as well as to observe the color of reflected light. To use the photometer, hold it up to brightly colored objects (clothes, folders, posterboards) and see the color reflected.

Attachment 3
Colorful Candy: Descriptive Research

Hypothesis: _____

Research:

Number	Red	Orange	Yellow	Green	Brown	Blue
1						
2						
3						
4						
5						
6						

Results of the experiment: _____

_____

Evaluation of hypothesis: _____

_____

Attachment 4

Colorful Pursuit

Create the questions for one of the categories in a "Colorful Pursuit" game.

1. Choose a color.
2. Brainstorm things associated with that color, use the dictionary or encyclopedia to create questions with answers that relate to the color.
   Example: Topic – Red
   Question: This little girl met the wolf on her way to Grandma's house.
   Answer: Little *Red* Riding Hood.
   Question: Who were referred to as the *Red* Coats during the American Revolutionary War?
   Answer: The British.
3. Use the computer to print your questions and answers.
4. Get an envelope from the teacher to store your cards in your portfolio.
5. Create a game board for your "Colorful Pursuit" game. Share your cards with others in the class and get copies of their questions.

Attachment 5

- **Realist:** Tries to paint scenes as they really look, true to the appearance of reality.

- **Expressionist:** Exaggerates or distorts the subject of the painting according to inner feelings and emotions.

- **Abstract Expressionist:** Chooses to paint in an explosive style, flinging paint on the canvas in a way that looks like it was accidental.

- **Surrealist:** An artist who finds the ideas for paintings in dreams and fantasies.

- **Social Realist:** An artist whose paintings point out and comment on the ills of society.

- **Cubist:** An artist who searches for basic geometric forms in nature and reorganizes them in new constructions.

- **Pop Artist:** An artist who uses the images of comic books, billboards, and the supermarket to make art that reflects our popular and commercial culture.

- **Op Artist:** An artist who paints in optical illusions that make use of the sciences of color and optics to dazzle the eye.

Attachment 6
Create a Center Sheet
Type of Art

1. _____ is ...

2. Some _____ artists are:

Directions: Create a(an) _____ drawing/ painting.

Your subject for this masterpiece should be _____.

You may use the following medium: _____

Group Members: _____

Unit 4
Measure Up to the Olympics

Areas of Giftedness
- Creativity
- General Intellectual Ability
- Leadership
- Specific Academic Area
  - Math

Grade Level
3

Duration
6 weeks

Generalizations
- We use systems to organize the acquisition and exchange of knowledge.
- There are many different systems.
- Systems aid in the collection of data to solve problems.
- In systems, the parts in concert total more than the sum of the separate parts.
- Systems work to complete a task or a mission.
- Exploring systems improves our understanding.

Theme:
Systems

Grade Level:
3

Developer:
Lynda Falconer

Objective	Activities	Interdisciplinary Connections
• In the study of measurement, students will investigate measurement tools and systems of the past and present.	• **Brainstorm all the ways you use measurement.**	• Math, Science
	• **Group the ways you use measurement into categories. Create a title for each category and record your ideas on butcher paper. Post your list on the wall.**	
	• **As a class, discuss the categories chosen by each group. Synthesize the information into a class chart of things that are measured. Use your findings to discover that time, length, capacity, mass, and temperature can be measured using the metric or customary system of measurement.**	
	• **Collect measurement tools of the past and present to display in a measurement museum.**	• Social Studies
	• **Write a detailed description and history of each item on an index card to be included in the display.**	• Language Arts
	• **Choose a museum curator or committee to arrange the display.**	• Language Arts
	• **Train students to be museum docents and present the collection to visitors. Invite other classes to visit your museum.**	• Public Speaking
	• **Brainstorm all the things at the Olympics that might need to be measured.**	• Math, Science
	• **Olympic officials have called the world's greatest scientists to debate which system of measurement should be officially used for the games. Compare the metric and customary systems of measurement in a debate. Students assume the roles of world famous scientists and defend their positions.**	• Math, Public Speaking
• Students will create original products in a simulation of their community's successful bid for the Olympic Games.	• **Compose a letter to persuade the Olympic Committee to hold the next summer or winter games in your town.**	• Language Arts, Social Studies
	• **Design a logo and mascot for the Olympics to be held in your town.**	• Art
	• **Choose a theme for the games.**	
	• **Create an Olympic T-shirt. Investigate appropriate projects or charities in your community that need funding. Choose an organization or project to receive the profits from T-shirt sales. Present your decisions to a mock city council. Justify your choices and explain the significance of the symbolism in your designs in a written report.**	• Social Studies, Language Arts

Authentic Methods and Context	Resources	Assessment
	• Large paper for brainstorming.	• Teacher observation.
	• Collected tools for measurement.	
• Investigate the way museums collect, catalog, and display items.		• Teacher observation.
• Interview a museum docent about the training and expertise required for his or her job.	• Museum curator and docent.	
		• Student/teacher-made rubric.
• Investigate community strengths and capacity to host large events through the Chamber of Commerce.	• Local Chamber of Commerce.	• Holistic scoring rubric to include number of persuasive points and extent of research.
• Contact the city council, United Way, and specific local organizations about groups and projects that help your community.	• Local government, volunteer agencies, or charitable organizations.	• Report assessed with class or teacher-made rubric.

Objective	Activities	Interdisciplinary Connections
	• **You are a newspaper reporter covering the Olympics. A terrible storm has blocked out all TV and radio communication. Only the mail can can get through. Write a news report telling the world about what is happening at the Olympics. Watch the Olympics on TV or make up a realistic simulation of your favorite event. Be sure to include the five W's (who, what, when, where, why).**	• Language Arts
• Students will plan and organize a mock Measurement Olympics in which students will measure length, mass, capacity, volume, time, and area to solve problems.	• **Prepare and present a welcome speech for the opening ceremony of the Measurement Olympics to be held in your town.**	• Public Speaking
	• **After studying the Olympic Pledge, compose a Measurement Olympics Pledge for team members to recite at the opening ceremony.**	• Language Arts
	• **In groups, choose the country you will represent. Research your country and design an appropriate uniform to wear at the opening ceremony. Create a flag for your country to carry.**	• Social Studies
	• **Create a mock-Olympic event for your classroom in which a metric measurement can be used to determine a winner. Name your event and design a medal for it. Write a description of your event.**	• Math, Science, Language Arts
	• **Design an Olympic TV directory for your local newspaper by converting Monday's Olympic Event schedule to central standard time. (See Attachment 1, page 40.)**	• Math, Science
• Students will explore the need for a standard system of measurement.	• **Measure the width of your desk with the tip of your index finger.**	• Math, Science
	• **Post your measurement on a class chart and compare your results to those of your classmates. Repeat the procedure using a centimeter ruler. Discuss the advantages of a standard unit of measurement.**	• Math
	• **Research the history of the standard measures we use now.**	• Social Studies
	• **Design and illustrate a poster depicting the origin of a measurement unit.**	• Math, Art
	• **Invent a new standard unit for measuring length. Design and construct a measuring tool that uses this standard unit. Give your standard unit a name and determine your height in your new unit. Create a magazine ad or TV commercial to advertise your new measuring tool.**	• Language Arts

Authentic Methods and Context	Resources	Assessment
	• Cole, A., Haas, C., Heller, E., & Weinberger, B. (1978). *Children are children are children*. Boston, MA: Little Brown.	
• Utilize travel guides and reference materials to understand the customs and daily lifestyle of people from another country.		• Teacher observation of participation and authenticity, completed pledges and flags.
	• AIMS Education Foundation. (1987). *Math + science = a solution*. Fresno, CA: Author.	• Completed event based on rubric designed by teacher and students.
	• Activity sheet.	• Activity sheet.
	• Centimeter ruler.	
		• Peer evaluation based on creativity and effectiveness of ad using a student or teacher-designed rubric.

Objective	Activities	Interdisciplinary Connections
• Students will use measurement skills to prepare for and compete in the Measurement Olympics.	• **Be a "suitcase scavenger." Choose your favorite Olympic event. Imagine that you are an athlete going to the Olympics to represent the USA in that event. Form a group with other teammates who have chosen the same event. What might you pack in your suitcase?**	• Language Arts
	• **Name an object for each length given on Attachment 2 (page 41). Choose only objects that can be found at home or in the classroom. Measure the longest side of each object and find the difference between the given measurement and the actual.**	• Math
See Lesson Plan 1, Below	• **Research the weather at the site of the next Olympic games. Compare the weather to that in your town. Plan and present a television weather forecast from both your town and the Olympic site. Include visual aids and consider details such as proper clothing and accent.**	
	• **Use estimation and measurement to compete in the Mini-Metric Olympics.**	• Math, Science

Lesson Plan 1

Measure Up to the Olympics
Measurement Skills

Lesson Objectives

Students will use measurement skills to solve problems in the Measurement Olympics.

Prerequisite Skills

This is the culminating activity for the unit. Students will need to have an understanding of the concepts of length, mass, capacity, and area and have had practice using tools to find these measure-

ments. Parts of this lesson may have been completed in prior sessions. These instructions cover several class periods of student preparation and the final event.

Materials

Math + Science = Solution; this book contains much background about the Olympics as well as blacklines of medals.

Children Are Children Are Children.

Introduction

Brainstorm memories of the opening ceremony of the Olympic Games. Discuss the preparation that went into the

planning of the games and the opening ceremony.

Activity Descriptions

1. Divide students into teams of up to 4 members. Each team will select a team captain. The team captain will draw a card to determine the country their team will represent in the Measurement Olympics.
2. After needed research, teams will construct a flag of their country to be carried in the opening ceremony.
3. Teams will prepare a short speech for the opening ceremony. In the speech,

Authentic Methods and Context	Resources	Assessment
• Students must plan what they will take on a trip abroad. Contact local airlines for luggage limits. Contact travel agents for suggestions for the country to which you are traveling.	• Travel Agencies, Airlines.	• Activity sheet.
		• Group and individual assessment: students describe the strengths and weaknesses of their group's preparation and final presentation. List things to improve.
• Students estimate, then measure the distances of paper straw javelins, cotton ball shot puts, and paper plate discuses are thrown in centimeters. Other activities include: marble grab mass, foot area, and sponge squeeze water volume.	• *Math + Science = Solution.* AIMS Education Foundation, 1987.	• Participation checklist. Teacher interview.

the country will say, "Hello," in their native language, express their gratitude for being invited to participate, show the location of their country on the globe, and tell 3 interesting facts about their country. The host country will include the same components in their speech, except they will welcome the competitors to their country.

4. Teams will design a simple team uniform to wear for the opening ceremony.

5. On the day of the Measurement Olympics, students, wearing their team uniforms, will parade into the opening ceremonies behind their country's flag. The host country will begin and give their welcoming speech. Other countries will follow in turn.

6. All students will compete in each of the 7 events. A large block of time may be set aside for this special day or the competition may be divided into several days with trial rounds of 2 to 3 events set up each day. Students may then rotate to compete. After all events have been completed, "judges" (parent helpers or students) will select the top 6 scorers in each event to compete in the finals. In all events, Olympians must first estimate the measure they expect to achieve. The competitor's score is the difference between his or her estimate and the actual measure. (See Attachment 3, page 42.)

7. The final competition is usually held on a different day. Teams may want to make signs to cheer on their teammates. At the end of each event final, the top 3 scorers will be pre-

sented homemade medals, while their countries' flags are raised and appropriate music is played.

To make awards: Copy the event medals (or let students design their own) onto gold, silver, and bronze paper. Laminate the medals and attach ribbons to each. Write the winner's name on each medal. Be sure to include the student-designed medal for the student-created event.

Closure

Students write about their experience in a math Olympic journal. Discuss what was learned about measurement, other countries, and working in a group. Evaluate and discuss what they liked most about the project and what they would change.

Extensions

Make a new design with the Olympic rings. Explain its meaning.

Play, "I Have ... Who Has?" to choose appropriate units of measure for various items or to convert measures within the same system.

Assessment

Students will self-evaluate the project through their journal writing. The project will be assessed by a rubric that incorporates instructor and student chosen criteria.

Attachment 1

Timely Olympians

It's time for the Olympics! Pretend that at 8 a.m. in your town, it is 2 a.m. the same day at the Olympics. The local newspaper has asked you to convert the Olympic schedule to your local time so that local viewers can watch the events live on TV. Design a TV schedule for the newspaper to list the local times for each event. Be sure to list the correct day of the week.

Mondays Event Schedule

- Men's Speed Skating—7 a.m.
- Women's Speed Skating—7:30 a.m.
- Bobsled—10:15 a.m.
- Luge—12:20 p.m.
- Women's Downhill—2:20 p.m.
- Pairs Skating—6:30 p.m.

Attachment 2

Choose your favorite Olympic event. Pretend you are going to the Olympics to compete in that event. Find items at home that you would pack in your suitcase that you estimate might have the following measurements. Record your estimate, then find the exact measurement. Find the difference between your estimate and the exact measure. Total the difference between the two measurements.

	Find Objects of These Lengths:	Name of Object	Actual Measurement	Difference
1	87 cm			
2	40 cm			
3	1 m			
4	3 cm			
5	31 cm			
6	1.5 m			
7	65 mm			
8	240 mm			
9	2 mm			
10	28 cm			

Attachment 3

In all events, Olympians must first estimate the measurement they expect to achieve. The competitor's score is the difference between his or her estimate and the actual measure.

Minimetric Olympics Score Sheet

Competitor _____

Team Captain _____

	Estimate	Actual	Score (difference)
1. **Paper Plate Discus Throw:** Throw a paper plate discus-style from the starting line. Measure the distance between the starting line and the closest edge of the plate in centimeters.	cm	cm	
2. **Paper Straw Javelin Throw:** Throw a paper straw javelin-style from the starting line. Measure the distance between the starting line and the closest edge of the straw in centimeters.	cm	cm	
3. **Cotton Ball Shot Put:** Toss a cotton ball shot put-style from the starting line. Measure the distance between the starting line and the closest edge in centimeters.	cm	cm	
4. **Right-Handed Marble Grab:** Reach your right hand into a bucket of marbles and grab as many as you can. Measure the weight of the marbles on a scale in grams.	g	g	
5. **Left-Handed Sponge Squeeze:** Using your left hand, dip a sponge into a bucket of water. Squeeze as much water as you can into a graduated cylinder in 15 seconds. Measure the amount of water in the cylinder in millimeters.	ml	ml	
6. **Big Foot Contest:** Trace your bare foot on centimeter graph paper. Find the area of your footprint by counting the squares. Have a judge approve your total. Measure the area of your footprint in square centimeters.	cm²	cm²	
7. **Student-Created Event:** Put a student's event description here.			

Total _____

Unit 5
You Don't Say!

Areas of Giftedness
- Creativity
- General Intellectual Ability
- Leadership
- Specific Academic Area
  - Math

Grade Level

3

Duration

9 Weeks (Pullout)

Generalizations
- People communicate to express their feelings and beliefs.
- People express themselves in a variety of ways.

Theme:
Communication

Grade Level:
3

Developer:
Julie Seymour

Objective	Activities	Interdisciplinary Connections
• In their study of folktales from around the world, students will analyze several to determine their purpose and compare them to scientific explanations.	• **Brainstorm types of literature.** • **Hypothesize as to why each were written.** • **Summarize a variety of folktales and myths, categorizing their purposes.** • **Research our culture's scientific explanation of a natural phenomenon and compare it to a folktale's explanation.**	• Language Arts, Social Studies
• Students will synthesize an original myth based on a science fiction story.	• **Analyze and interpret a science fiction story.** • **Create an original myth to explain how this story could have occurred.**	• Language Arts
• Students will analyze the composition and art elements of the illustrations of the myths to determine mood and create an original work reflecting an emotion and an aspect of culture.	• **Analyze and classify illustrations from folktale books according to mood depicted.** • **Isolate artistic elements that created various moods (i.e. line, color, form, etc.).** • **Identify parts of culture that were depicted in the artwork.** • **Create unique artwork reflecting an emotion and an aspect of our culture.**	• Art, Social Studies
• In their study of various types of communication, students will analyze several types of number systems from throughout history to determine similarities and differences. See Lesson Plan 1, Page 48	• **Analyze illustrations from *The Golden Flower* to isolate any other forms of communication depicted in pictures, particularly hieroglyphics.** • **Research and study the Egyptian hieroglyphic number system and apply it to various situations.** • **Research and compare the ancient Egyptian number system with those of other early civilizations.** • **Compare and contrast Egyptian and Roman numeral systems.** • **Compare and evaluate Egyptian, Roman, and Hindu-Arabic number systems.**	• Social Studies, Math, Language Arts

Authentic Methods and Context	Resources	Assessment
	• Various folktales from around the world. • Craig-Palazzo, J. (1997). *Tam's slipper*. Troll. • Craig-Palazzo, J. (1997). *Why spider spins tales*. Troll. • Craig-Palazzo, J. (1999). *The magic peach*. Troll. • Craig-Palazzo, J. (1997). *The golden flower: A story of Egypt*. Troll. • Newton-Chocolate, D. (1993). *Talk, talk*. Troll.	• Folktale summaries will be evaluated by students using predetermined criteria. • Venn diagram of folktale purposes will be evaluated by the teacher based on teacher-selected criteria of story purposes.
	• Roman myth, "Chariot of the Sun God." • Graphic organizer to record story summaries. • Venn diagram to categorize purposes of stories. • Various reference materials (CD ROMs, encyclopedias, nonfiction books, Internet sites).	• Completed research with optional oral presentation.
• Have students interview fiction authors about how they develop plot. Research past science fiction writings to find out if it is now reality. • Listen to a local artist convey how his or her artwork is influenced by cultural aspects. Receive input on individually-created artwork.	• Asimov, I. (1984). How now purple cow. In: *Fantastic reading: Stories and activities for grades 5–8*. Pacific Palisades, CA: Goodyear Publishing. • Books listed above. • Attachments 4 & 5, pages 54–55. • Assorted art materials.	• Original student work to be evaluated by class for clarity, creativity, and written style. • Completed art product will be evaluated by a teacher-created grid utilizing student and teacher-selected criteria.
	• Craig-Palazzo, J. (1997). *The golden flower: A story of Egypt*. Troll. • Various sources of information on ancient number systems. • T-chart to identify similarities and differences between number systems.	• Completed a graphic organizer to classify similarities and differences of ancient number systems will be evaluated using teacher-selected criteria on a rubric.

Objective	Activities	Interdisciplinary Connections
• In their study of how people communicate information differently, students will analyze scientific notation and the number system and translate it into base ten Arabic numerals.	• **Demonstrate the translation of number values into scientific notation.** • **Investigate the binary number system used in computers.**	• Math, Science
• In their study of how people communicate through the science and art of architecture, students will analyze the structural form and function of design of various buildings and synthesize an original design.	• **Brainstorm a list of buildings from the area. Determine purpose of various features of the structures.** • **Analyze photos of buildings from Washington, DC, and hypothesize as to the message the architect wished to reflect.** • **Analyze a timeline of architecture and determine how function and form have changed over the past 1000 years. Hypothesize as to why these changes occurred.** • **Plan and create a unique structure for today, defining a specific purpose and reflecting an an appropriate feeling. Be sure to use accurate scale in the diagram.**	• Social Studies, Art, Math
• In their study of the human need to communicate, students will identify a personal need to express and create an original message in the medium of their choice. See Lesson Plan 2, Page 52	• **Interpret "The Road Not Taken" by Robert Frost and relate his message of risk-taking to his profession as a poet.** • **Brainstorm a list of ways that people have communicated and the messages they have communicated.** • **Formulate criteria and apply them to decide upon student's personal message and medium of choice to create.** • **Create original student message in medium of choice.**	• Language Arts, Social Studies, Art

Authentic Methods and Context	Resources	Assessment
• Discover different needs and forms for communicating information by visiting one or more of the following: Scout Leaders (Morse Code), baseball pitchers, and military signal experts.		• Results of translation of values into scientific notation and the base ten system will be evaluated by teacher-selected criteria.
• Present created structure to an architect to analyze its purpose/feelings and scale its accuracy.	• D'Alelio, J. (1989). *I know that building!*. Washington, DC: The Preservation Press: National Trust for Historic Preservation.	• Evaluate the unique structures created based on criteria on a teacher/student-designed rubric.
	• Frost, R. (1920). The road not taken. *Mountain interval.* New York: Henry Holt & Company.	• Completed student message will be self-evaluated using a teacher and student-selected criteria on an evaluation checklist.

Lesson Plan 1

You Don't Say!
Number Systems

Lesson Objectives

In their study of various types of communication, students will analyze several types of number systems from throughout history to determine similarities and differences.

Prerequisite Skills

Understanding how people communicate in various ways, understanding the use of graphic organizers, ease of use in base ten counting system.

Materials

The Golden Flower: A Story From Egypt; Attachment 1, page 49; Attachment 2, page 51.

Introduction

Ask students to determine the number of folktales that they have discussed during this unit. Discuss how they have communicated this result (numerically).

Begin a discussion that centers around what types of things numbers are used to communicate. Then, review with the class the information found at the end of the book, *The Golden Flower: A Story From Egypt.* Highlight the fact that the pharaoh depicted in the story ruled Egypt about the same time that the first number system was developed there. It was a hieroglyph system. Analyze the illustrations in the text to see if the students can identify any hieroglyphs.

Activity Descriptions

1. Direct the students to analyze the hieroglyphic numeration system shown on the "It All Adds Up" activity page (Attachment 1, page 49). Complete the computation for the first of the hieroglyphs from King Narmer's mace-head. (Note: You read the larger numbers from right to left.) Have students complete the other two as they become more proficient at it. Discuss the meanings of the markings for each sample. Then, have the students complete the rest of the sheet independently.

2. Next, have the students analyze the examples of other early number systems, discussing their similarities and differences. (Attachment 2, page 51.) Note that they are additive in nature, that is, they add symbols to designate a certain value. Highlight the fact that at certain numbers (usually 4 or 5) the hieroglyphs regrouped. Ask students to speculate why this was. (To keep track when counting—it is visually difficult to differentiate the amounts beyond a string of 4 marks.) As a group, compare and contrast the similarities between these number systems.

Closure

Create a T-bar or other type of graphic organizer to record these ideas.

Extensions

Have students research other types of number systems, comparing their date of origin and symbolism used with those systems previously discussed.

Assessment

Have students rank the number systems from most to least symbolic, having them cite reasons for their choices.

Attachment 1
It All Adds Up

The Egyptians, under the rule of Senefru, were among the first people to use a written number system. Their numbers looked like this:

	Units	Tens	Hundreds	Thousands	Ten Thousands	Hundred Thousands
1	＿	∩	ℓ	𐦜	∅	🦅
2	＝	∩∩	ℓℓ	𐦜𐦜	∅∅	🦅🦅
3	≡	∩∩∩	ℓℓℓ	𐦜𐦜𐦜	∅∅∅	🦅🦅🦅
4	＝＝	∩∩∩∩	ℓℓℓℓ	𐦜𐦜𐦜𐦜	∅∅∅∅	🦅🦅🦅🦅
5	≡＝	∩∩∩∩∩	ℓℓℓℓℓ	𐦜𐦜𐦜𐦜𐦜	∅∅∅∅∅	🦅🦅🦅🦅🦅
6	≡≡	∩∩∩∩∩∩	ℓℓℓℓℓℓ	𐦜𐦜𐦜𐦜𐦜𐦜	∅∅∅∅∅∅	🦅🦅🦅🦅🦅🦅
7	≡≡＝	∩∩∩∩∩∩∩	ℓℓℓℓℓℓℓ	𐦜𐦜𐦜𐦜𐦜𐦜𐦜	∅∅∅∅∅∅∅	🦅🦅🦅🦅🦅🦅🦅
8	≡≡≡	∩∩∩∩∩∩∩∩	ℓℓℓℓℓℓℓℓ	𐦜𐦜𐦜𐦜𐦜𐦜𐦜𐦜	∅∅∅∅∅∅∅∅	🦅🦅🦅🦅🦅🦅🦅🦅
9	≡≡≡＝	∩∩∩∩∩∩∩∩∩	ℓℓℓℓℓℓℓℓℓ	𐦜𐦜𐦜𐦜𐦜𐦜𐦜𐦜𐦜	∅∅∅∅∅∅∅∅∅	🦅🦅🦅🦅🦅🦅🦅🦅🦅

Attachment 1—Continued

Here is a sample of the Egyptian numbers from 1–9. Compare these to other examples of early numbers that other people developed. Number them from the least symbolic to the most symbolic.

Egyption Numbers

Summerian Numbers

Ancient Elamite Numbers

Aztec Numbers

Ancient Greek Numbers

Mayan Numbers

Attachment 2

Comparing and Contrasting
Ancient Number Systems

Similarities	Differences

This is a carving from King Narmer's mace-head that showed how many items he claimed after a victorious expedition. Write the number of bulls, goats, and prisoners that were taken below each picture using our number system.

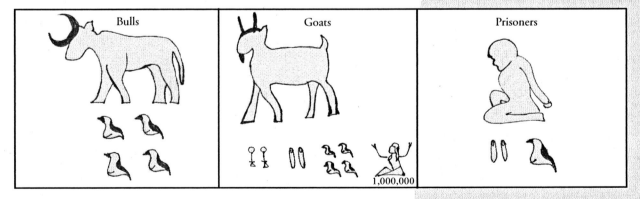

Lesson Plan 2

You Don't Say!
Communicating

Lesson Objectives

In their study of the human need to communicate, students will identify a personal need to express and create an original message in the medium of their choice.

Prerequisite Skills

Understanding how people communicate in various ways, how basic elements of art produce mood and emotion, decision-making skills (see Attachment 5, page 55), critical reading skills, and understanding of graphic organizers.

Materials

"The Road Not Taken" by Robert Frost; Attachment 3, page 53; Attachment 4, page 54; Attachment 5, page 55; and various materials for product creation.

Introduction

Interpret Robert Frost's poem, "The Road Not Taken," using the graphic organizer. Relate his message of risk-taking to his profession as a poet. You may wish to bring in other forms of communication (music, painting, etc.) so that students can determine the message and mood of each piece.

Activity Descriptions

1. Have students brainstorm a list of ways that people communicate and the messages they have communicated (commercials, newspapers, poetry, computer programs, art, music, dance, and so forth).
2. Instruct students that they will be choosing a message that has personal significance to them and the means in which to communicate it. Have the students apply criteria to aide them as they choose their message and form of communication. You may wish to model two criteria and have the students create a third on their own.
3. Students will then develop a plan and "construct" their message.

Closure

Students will present their finished product to the class, incorporating good public speaking skills.

Extensions

Students may attend a fine arts function (art museum display, musical, etc.) and evaluate the production to determine mood and message, as well as critique the elements of the work.

Assessment

Have students evaluate each others' products based on predetermined criteria.

Attachment 3
Understanding the "Road" Signs

First, read the title to interpret a poem. What idea do you expect to see repeated throughout the writing? Circle that in the center circle of the web. Read the entire poem, then go back and study each verse separately. Fill in the web by writing the major ideas of each verse (look for nouns and verbs, then adjectives and adverbs to describe them).

Student

Verse 1

Verse 2

"The Road
Not Taken"

Verse 3

Verse 4

Teacher's Notes

Road two
woods
as far as I could
Verse 1 Looked to it bent
into undergrowth
sorry couldn't
travel both
traveler

Other Road
grassy wanted wear
Verse 2
about the
same as other
Worn

"The Road
Not Taken"

equally lay
No Leaves both roads
not trodden black
Verse 3

doubted I should be back
Way Leads on to Way

with a sigh
Telling
ages and ages hence
Verse 4

less traveled
Took the one
made all the difference

53

Attachment 4
Hear Me Roar

The first thing a good communicator develops is the message. Your purpose and ideas must be clear. The more important they are to you, the better your chances are at communicating them. Brainstorm a list of ideas that are important to you that you would like to share. It could be about family, school, play, the world, your beliefs, and so forth.

_____

_____

_____

_____

_____

_____

Complete the criteria chart and circle the message above that you will be trying to communicate. Now that you have a message, you need to brainstorm ways to communicate it.

_____

_____

_____

_____

_____

_____

Complete the criteria chart and circle the form of communication above that you will be producing. Briefly describe how you will create your message.

_____

_____

_____

_____

_____

_____

Attachment 5

Hear Me Roar

Message Choices	Criteria I	Criteria II	Criteria III

Criteria:
1.
2.
3.

Message Choices	Criteria I	Criteria II	Criteria III

Criteria:
1.
2.
3.

Unit 6
My Lights

Areas of Giftedness
- Creative Thinking
- General Intellectual Ability
- Specific Academic Area
  - Language Arts

Grade Levels

3–6

Duration

12–15 Weeks (Pullout)
6–9 Weeks (Cluster)

Generalizations
- Authentic writing assignments enhance quality of student work.
- Ownership of work products increases motivation and fosters independence and creative thinking.
- Ideas can be communicated through a variety of writing styles.
- Publishing a magazine is a process of inter-related steps that build upon each other.

**Theme:
Communication**

**Grade Levels:
3–6**

**Developers:
Kristen Norton
and
Phyllis Ducote**

Objective	Activities	Interdisciplinary Connections
• By creating original magazines, students will apply what they have learned about publishing and the writing process to establish publishing guidelines. See Lesson Plan 1, Page 60	• Read children's magazines such as *Highlights* and *Cricket* to understand the format and to help generate ideas. • Brainstorm components of a publishable magazine and use them to establish a checklist for their own magazine components. • Establish a range of financial values for each type of writing (i.e., a biographical piece may be worth $8–$12, while a crossword puzzle may be worth $3–$5). • Read about and discuss the publishing process for books and magazines. • Review components of the writing process including prewriting, drafting, revising, elaboration, editing, and publishing.	• Language Arts, Science, Social Studies
• Students will write original articles using a variety of genres that are employed in children's magazines.	• Review elements of each type of writing including biography, fantasy, realistic fiction, nonfiction, poetry, etc. • Work independently to write articles on topics of students' choice that will meet the requirements set forth in the checklist. • Research article topics using a variety of reference materials and Internet sites.	• Language Arts, Science, Social Studies
• Students will learn the "value" of a piece of writing.	• Arrange conferences between author (student) and publisher (teacher) to discuss, edit, and purchase student work for prices established on the checklist. • Revise and rewrite articles based on conferences with publisher. • These steps are repeated over a period of several weeks.	• Language Arts, Math
• Students will design magazine layouts and create artwork to enhance articles by incorporating visual arts.	• Organize publishable pieces into a magazine layout. • Design front and back cover for magazine. • Illustrate articles using both original and computer-generated artwork.	• Language Arts, Art
• Students will calculate the total amount of money earned in the publication of their magazines and share their final products.	• Keep track of the amount of money students have earned by selling articles and art to the publisher. • Spend their money to buy items offered by the publisher at regular intervals (lower priced items might include rubber balls and plastic rings and cars; higher-priced items might include going out to lunch with the teacher). • Each student will select one article to share at a formal reading for parents, lower grade levels, or both. • Display students' magazines in the school library.	• Language Arts, Math

Authentic Methods and Context	Resources	Assessment
	• *Highlights for Children.* • *Cricket.* Carus Publishing Company. • *Storyworks.* Scholastic. • Nixon, J.L. (1988). *If you were a writer.* New York: Four Winds Press.	• Teacher observation of class participation. • Teacher approval of student checklists.
	• Thomson, R. (1988). *Making a book.* New York: Watts.	
• Writing for a real audience.	• Slack, C. (1993). *Foundation for writing.* ECS Learning Systems, Inc. • Slack, C. (1995). *Foundation for writing, Book II.* ECS Learning Systems, Inc.	
	• Kranz, R. (n.d.). *Write on!.* Troll Associates. • Greene, C. (1988). *How a book is made.* Chicago, IL: Children's Press.	• Teacher and student will negotiate value of each piece of writing submitted.
• Visit a graphic arts specialist to gain insight and feedback on design layouts.	• Kids' Stuff (Eds.). (2002). *Writing yellow pages for students and teachers.* Nashville, TN: Incentive Publications, Inc. • Frank, M. (1995). *If you're trying to teach kids how to write, you gotta have this book.* Nashville, TN: Incentive Publications, Inc.	• Teacher and student will negotiate value of each piece of art submitted. • Teacher will evaluate final products using the checklist established at the beginning of the unit.

Lesson Plan 1

My Lights
Magazine Publishing

Lesson Objectives

By creating original magazines, students will apply what they have learned about publishing and the writing process to establish publishing guidelines.

Prerequisite Skills

Understand all elements of the writing process. Understand the value of money.

Materials

Children's magazines like *Highlights, Cricket,* and *Storyworks.*

Introduction

Explain to students that they will create their own magazines.

Introduce various children's magazines and allow students sufficient time to read and explore several different ones.

Activity Descriptions

1. Discuss magazines including likes and dislikes of specific articles and pieces.
2. Brainstorm categories of magazine entries and list them on butcher paper (i.e., fiction, nonfiction, puzzles, etc.).
3. List different components of each category. For nonfiction, components might be biographies, science articles, social studies articles, how-to articles, and so forth.
4. Establish a range of financial values for each type of writing (i.e., a biographical piece may be worth $8–$12, while a crossword puzzle may be worth $3–$5).
5. Have students create a proposed checklist of components for their own magazine which will include at least four major articles (fiction or nonfiction) and six minor pieces (poems, recipes, cartoons, puzzles, ads, etc.).
6. Discuss the publishing process as it relates to the purchasing of written work by the publisher (teacher).

Closure

Compare their checklist to previously read magazines to see if they have similar components; turn in the checklist for teacher approval.

Extensions

Read additional magazines for fun and for ideas.

Notes

Unit 7
Up, Up, and Away!

Areas of Giftedness
- General Intellectual Ability
- Specific Academic Areas
  - Creative Thinking
  - Fine Arts
  - Language Arts
  - Science
  - Social Studies

Grade Levels

3–5

Duration

4–6 Weeks

Generalizations
- Making connections to aviation history promotes understanding of the present state of aviational developments.
- Exploring the relationships of aerodynamic principles encourages universal connections.
- Connections exist between alternative aircraft and future developments.

Theme:
Connections

Grade Levels:
3–5

Developer:
Cheri Strange

Objective	Activities	Interdisciplinary Connections
• During the study of aviation history, students will incorporate research to design a variety of original products.	• **Determine prior knowledge of aviation by completing the K (what I *know*) and W (what I *want* to know) parts of a KWL chart.**	• Language Arts
	• **After hearing the myth of Icarus and Daedalus, students create their own original legend about the beginning of flight.**	• Language Arts, Social Studies
	• **Become familiar with historical developments of flight. Create a visual timeline, illustrating important events and places of flight history in chronological order.**	• Language Arts, Social Studies
	• **Hypothesize who the first aerial passengers were. Discuss and relate how balloons are used in military defense.**	• Language Arts, Social Studies
	• **Research the first space passengers.**	• Language Arts
	• **Compare types of aircraft, noting changes and improvements.**	• Language Arts, Science
	• **Brainstorm ways aircraft of today can be improved.**	• Language Arts
	• **After analyzing the information concerning Navy blimp Airship L-8, students work in groups to create a segment for *Unsolved Mysteries*.**	• Language Arts, Art
	• **Brainstorm the personality traits of an aviator. Write a personal profile of a pilot.**	• Social Studies, Language Arts
	• **Compare and contrast the personal characteristics needed to be an early aviator versus a modern-day aviator.**	• Language Arts, Social Studies
	• **Research a historical flight. Recreate an imaginary flight log for the flight.**	• Language Arts, Social Studies
	• **Design a commemorative stamp celebrating an important event or person in aviation.**	• Language Arts, Social Studies
• In their study of flight, the students will examine alternative aircraft and distinguish similarities and differences. See Lesson Plan 1, Page 66	• **Simulate historic around-the-world flights and study the principles of mapmaking by inventing an original board game.**	• Language Arts, Social Studies
	• **Investigate hydrogen and hot air balloons. Create papier-mâché models of these balloons displaying differences and similarities.**	• Language Arts, Science

Authentic Methods and Context	Resources	Assessment
		• Teacher observations.
	• Abate, R. (n.d.). *The history of airplanes.* La Sorgente Publishing. • Gilleo, A. (1977). *Air travel from the beginning.* Chicago, IL: Children's Press. • Dean, A. (1980). *Up, up, and away! The story of balloons.* Philadelphia, PA: Westminster Press.	• Teacher and students will generate rubric criteria for evaluation of original products. • Teacher observations.
	• Dwiggins, D. (1982). *Flying the frontiers of space.* New York: Dodd, Mead & Co. • Taylor, J.W.R. (1970). *Aircraft, aircraft.* London: Hamlyn.	• Teacher and student will generate rubric criteria for evaluation of original products.
• Interview a pilot from the community.	• Dolan, E.F. (1983). *Great mysteries of the air.* New York: Dodd, Mead, & Co. • http://www.friendshipflight.com. • Madison, A. (1977). *Aviation careers.* New York: Franklin Watts. • Lindbergh, C. (1998). *The spirit of St. Louis.* New York: Charles Scribner's Sons.	
	• http://www.multied.com/AVChron.html. • Kershner, W. (2003). *The advanced pilots flight manual.* Ames: Iowa State University.	• Teacher observations. • Teacher and student will generate rubric criteria for evaluation of products.

Objective	Activities	Interdisciplinary Connections
	• **Examine the similarities and differences between blimps and dirigibles.**	• Language Arts
	• **Generate "What Am I?" riddles about various types of alternative aircraft.**	• Science
	• **Create original poems pertaining to aviation and share with the class.**	• Language Arts
	• **Debate the pros and cons of gliders as compared airplanes.**	• Language Arts, Science
	• **Assume the role of a glider pilot. Students act out a scene in which they experience various conditions (clear skies, crowded air space, etc.). Explain the adjustments needed for each condition.**	• Language Arts, Art, Science
	• **Students demonstrate the four principles of flight (lift, gravity, thrust, and drag) by designing an exhibit based on all four.**	• Science
	• **Investigate the beginnings of NASA in relation to background, purpose, and influences on future problems.**	• Language Arts, Science
• Students will investigate and simulate various principles of flight to promote their understanding of aerodynamics.	• **Explore the principle of inertia.**	• Science

Authentic Methods and Context	Resources	Assessment
	• Dean, A. (1980). *Up, up, and away! The story of balloons*. Philadelphia, PA: Westminster Press.	
• Design and create prototypes of paper gliders. Invite a pilot to help students evaluate which attributes of the designs allow it to fly the farthest, highest, and so forth.	• Daniel, C., & Daniel, B. (1978). *The great paper airplane factory*. Good Apple, Inc. • Feravolo, R.V. (1960). *Junior science book of flying*. Champaign, IL: Garrard Press.	• Teacher observations.
		• Teacher and student will generate rubric criteria for evaluation of original products.
	• NASA: http://spaceflight.nasa.gov.	
• Correspond with NASA through e-mail to discover what steps could be taken to allow a student to travel on a space shuttle mission. • Visit an air field in which students can explore radar, approach control, control tower, and flight simulators. Students assist in securing the day's flight plan.	• Corbett, S. (1967). *What makes a plane fly?*. Boston, MA: Little, Brown, & Co. • NASA: http://spaceflight.nasa.gov. • Any local air base or airport.	• Teacher observations.

Lesson Plan 1

Up, Up, and Away!
Aircraft Simulations

Lesson Objectives
Through simulations, students will examine alternative aircraft and distinguish similarities and differences.

Prerequisite Skills
Some background information on the evolution of aircraft.

Materials
Illustrations of various balloons (hot air and hydrogen), strips of newspaper, glue, and various art supplies.

Introduction
Students begin with a key word given and brainstorm (diverge) all ideas that come to mind that are linked to the previous word. When time is called, they converge from the last word on the list back to the original word. (balloons, aircraft, flight)

Activity Descriptions
1. Discuss hydrogen and hot air balloons.
2. Study illustrations of various hot air and hydrogen balloons from available materials.
3. Compare and contrast hydrogen and hot air balloons in a Venn diagram.
4. Design a hydrogen and hot air balloon, paying close attention to details that demonstrate the similarities and differences between the two types of balloons.
5. Create papier-mâché models of the designs.
   a. Dip strips of newspaper into paste and place around an inflated balloon.
   b. After it has dried, pop the balloon by sticking it with a pin.
   c. Students decorate balloons with various mediums.
   d. Design and attach the car.
6. Working with a guest pilot, assess what changes should be made to devise the best paper glider.
7. Draw and describe a new and improved glider.
8. Construct this new design; field-test against other new and improved models.

Closure
Students discuss what they learned from designing and testing their gliders. Share positive findings and problems encountered with the prototypes and final designs.

Extensions
Students may name their improved glider and create an advertisement for their model.

Students debate the pros and cons of gliders as compared to airplanes.

Investigate people who make gliders as a hobby.

Assessment
Teacher, student, and peer evaluations are used in a rubric that incorporates criteria from all parties.

Unit 8
Out of the Dark: Castles & Knights

Areas of Giftedness
- General Intellectual Creativity
- Specific Academic Areas
  - Language Arts
  - Math
  - Social Studies

Grade Level
4

Duration
4–6 Weeks (Pullout)
2–4 Weeks (Cluster)

Generalizations
- Exploring relationships improves understanding.
- Relationships exist between past and present societies.
- Experiencing real-life situations improves problem solving.
- Exploration confronts "the unknown."
- Exploration requires leadership.
- Exploration may result in new findings.

**Theme:
Explorations**

**Grade Level:
4**

**Developers:
Shirley Sowels
and
Linda Ellis**

Objective	Activities	Interdisciplinary Connections
• Students will identify and differentiate between the Dark Ages and the Middle Ages using timelines and selected events.	• **Teacher introduction of the year 1348. The population of Europe was reduced from about 90 million to 60 million.** • **Students research events and dates to determine the possibility of their chosen event contributing to the reduction in population.** • **Investigate effects of Bubonic Plague.**	• Social Studies, Language Arts
• Compare/contrast physical boundaries of the maps of 1000 A.D. to maps of today.	• **Document differences in the contrasting maps.** • **Observe trends and draw conclusions from the map changes.** • **Present a documentary describing the geographical changes in the maps during this time period.**	• Social Studies
• By creating original products, students will apply what they have learned to demonstrate their understanding of societal rank and loyalties during the Dark and Middle Ages in Europe.	• **Investigate kinds of crops that were grown during the Middle Ages, feudalism, and manorialism and how the inventions of various farm tools aided the peasants.** • **Students debate the advantages and disadvantages of belonging to each class of societal rank.**	• Social Studies, Language Arts
• Identify components of a Medieval Castle and the surrounding village. See Lesson Plan 1, Page 70	• **Through use of resources, students locate the portcullis, drawbridge, moat, keep gatehouse, bailey, towers, courtyard, chapel, armory, and wall walk.** • **With the knowledge that one square of graph paper equals 10 square feet, students sketch outer walls of a castle that has a perimeter of 2,000 feet. The design must be a polygon with a minimum of five sides.** • **Design a floorplan of a castle. Required rooms are kitchen, chapel, great hall, master chamber, stairs inner bailey, garderobe, bedrooms, water closets, and other areas of choice. Include the perimeter and area of each room, as well as the purpose of the room.**	• English, Language Arts
• Original products will aid in determining the role of a knight in the feudal system and the order of steps to knighthood. Identify parts of knight armor and weapons. • Interpret opinions about life in the Middle Ages.	• **Research weapons used by knights and the steps knighthood.** • **Design and create a medieval weapon.** • **Brainstorm about Middle Ages lifestyle.** • **Design a personal coat of arms.**	• Social Studies
• Evaluate occupations and the apparel of castle residents and visitors.	• **Research clothing styles during the Middle Ages.** • **Create an employment application for specific jobs within a castle.**	• Social Studies, English, Language Arts
• Recognize the role of music, dance, and games in the lives of people living in a castle during the Middle Ages. See Lesson Plan 2, Page 70	• **Organize specialists who have researched kinds of games, music, and dances of the Middle Ages.** • **Recreate castle entertainment by performing dances or music reflective of the time.**	• Social Studies, English, Language Arts

Authentic Methods and Context	Resources	Assessment
• Investigate current research on deadly diseases, their causes, and the effect on the population and behavior.	• Fischer, M.W. (1995). *World history simulations.* Huntington Beach, CA: Teacher Created Materials, Inc. • McCarthy, T. (1996). *The Middle Ages: Stories activities, & reproducibles to connect reading and writing with social studies.* Scholastic Books.	• Teacher observation. Completed Research.
• Discover how boundary changes affect cities, governments, and schools.	• Pofahl, J. (1993). *Middle Ages: Knights and castles.* Minneapolis, MN: T.S. Dennison and Co.	• Teacher observation. Completed documentary.
• Investigate "defining roles" in today's world. Debate the benefits and and disadvantages.	• Pofahl, J. (1982). *Middle Ages: Personalities.* Minneapolis, MN: T. S. Dennison and Co.	• Student evaluation of debate using a student designed rubric.
• Experience the considerations of construction to blueprints by constructing a model from student sketches. Materials can vary.	• Sylvester, D. (1993). *Mythology, archaeology, architecture.* The Learning Works. • MacDonald, F. (1993). *Inside story: A medieval castle.* Bedrick Books.	• Product evaluation using a teacher or student-designed rubric.
	• Doherty, E., & Evans, L. (n.d.). *Just for fun.* East Windsor Hill, CT: Synergetics.	• Teacher Observation.
• Investigate the significance of symbolism in our culture. How would we be affected without it? • Investigate the differences in job requirements and applications for different areas of employment. Discover how education and experience affect job placement by employers in the community.	• Chorzempa, R. (1987). *Design your own coat of arms.* New York: Dover Publications. • Stangl, J. (1994). *Castles and fairy tales.* Minneapolis, MN: T.S. Dennison and Co.	• Teacher evaluation of of shields. • Teacher observation. Completed applications and investigations. • Teacher/student evaluation of performance based upon rubric.

Lesson Plan 1

Out of the Dark:
Castles and Knights
The Medieval Castle

Lesson Objectives
Student will identify components of a Medieval Castle and the surrounding village. Students will create a drawing of their own castle.

Prerequisite Skills
Understanding of perimeter and area.

Materials
Graph paper, books listed, and various building materials.

Introduction
Brainstorm about what things are essential to a castle.

Activity Descriptions
1. Through use of resources, students locate the portcullis, drawbridge, moat, keep gatehouse, bailey, towers, courtyard, chapel, armory, and wall walk.
2. With the knowledge that 1 square of graph paper equals 10 square feet, students sketch outer walls of a castle that has a perimeter of 2,000 feet. The design must be a polygon with a minimum of five sides.
3. Design a floor plan of a castle. Required rooms: kitchen, chapel, great hall, master chamber, stairs, four towers, inner bailey, garderobe, bedrooms, water closets, and any other areas of choice. Include the perimeter and areas of each room, as well as the purpose of the room.
4. Construct a model of the castle from sketch. Materials can vary. Suggestions: toothpicks, twigs, sand, sugar cubes, ice cream sticks, and clay.
5. You are a real estate agent. Write a real estate advertisement describing the castle's unique features and advantages. Convince someone to buy your castle.

Closure
Students share, discuss and evaluate products.

Extensions
Students decide which areas of the castle were used for offense and defense.

Assessment
Teacher evaluation of castle and advertisement using preset criteria.

Lesson Plan 2

Out of the Dark:
Castles and Knights
Medieval Music and Dance

Lesson Objectives
To recognize the role of music, dance, and games in the lives of people living in a castle during the Middle Ages.

Prerequisite Skills
Knowledge of occupations and clothing of people who lived in castles.

Materials
Books listed on page 69, music tape, games, and information.

Introduction
Brainstorm and categorize music, dance, and games that are used for entertainment today.

Activity Descriptions
1. Research the kinds of games, music, and dances of the Middle Ages.
2. Morris dance. Listen to taped music. Explain what a Morris dance is and how it is done. With some friends, learn and perform this dance at a banquet as part of the entertainment.
3. Jingle Activity. You are the court jester in charge of the entertainment for the

castle. You are to write one or more jingles that give information about some aspect of medieval life. Try and make your jingle catchy, the sort of rhyme others learn easily. Memorize your jingle and perform it at the banquet.

Closure

Students engage in a variety of entertainment for different classes of people from games, musicians, and story tellers.

Extensions

Compare the gambling of Medieval times to the lottery of today.

Round Robin Chess or Checkers tournament.

Assessment

Students memorize jingle and dance to be performed at a banquet. Evaluation of performance is based on a rubric.

Notes

Unit 9
To Tell the Truth:
Fairy Tale Character Analysis

Areas of Giftedness
- General Intellectual Creativity
- Specific Academic Area
  - Language Arts

Grade Levels
4–5

Duration
1–3 Weeks (Pullout)

Generalizations
- Analysis improves understanding of character motivations and interactions.
- Authors' opinions of their own characters are reflected in the details they provide.
- Writing an elaborated commentary on a character is facilitated by previously charting quotations and ideas.

Theme:
Truth and Justice

Grade Levels:
4–5

Developer:
Jan Cannon

Objective	Activities	Interdisciplinary Connections
• Using a rhetorical technique based on the analysis of quotations and accumulation of details, students will write a commentary on a character and draw conclusions on the author's treatment of the character. See Lesson Plan 1, Below	• **Read and review Perrault's fairy tales.** • **Select character and locate significant quotes affiliated with the character.** • **Brainstorm reasons for selecting quotes (commentary).** • **Locate other quotes related to the character and write commentaries for each.** • **Use the quotations and commentaries to write paragraphs analyzing the character. Combine the paragraphs to make an essay.** • **Repeat the process with other characters of the student's choice from the same fairy tale or another.** • **Create an illustrated book. Each page contains a selected quote illustrated with a full-page color picture.**	• Language Arts • Art

Lesson Plan 1

To Tell the Truth
Measurement Skills

Lesson Objectives
Using a rhetorical technique based on the analysis of quotations and accumulation of details, students will write a commentary on a character and draw conclusions on the author's treatment of the character.

Prerequisite Skills
Knowledge of essay structure and punctuation rules relating to the use of quotation marks.

Materials
The Random House Book of
Fairy Tales or other anthologies and a Character Chart Advance Organizer.

Introduction
Encourage students to name their favorite literary characters. After discussing why each character was chosen, guide students to speculate on how the characters' authors felt about these characters and about other characters with which the students are familiar, including a villain or two.

Activity Descriptions
1. Direct students to read Charles Perrault's "The Sleeping Beauty in the Wood."
2. On the chalkboard or overhead, write the following quotation: "She (the old fairy) had not been

invited because she had shut herself in a high, distant tower for many years and it was thought that she was dead."
3. Ask the students what they can tell about this particular fairy from the passage and what questions does the passage raise. Write their responses on the board, overhead, or a chart tablet. Possible answers:
   – The old fairy chose to be by herself for a long time.
   – She must have been important in the past or people wouldn't have been thinking about whether she was alive or dead.

   Questions raised include:
   – Why had she shut herself in the tower?

74

Authentic Methods and Context	Resources	Assessment
• As the reviewer for a newspaper or magazine, compose a response based on the author's treatment of a character in the book or story.	• Random House. (2000). *The Random House book of fairy tales*. New York: Author. • Character Chart Advance Organizer. • Advanced Placement English Workshop materials.	• Incremental assessment of each selected quote and commentary. • Paragraph assessment based on established rubrics. • Essay evaluated using district rubrics, TAKS writing guidelines or both.

— What happened that caused her to do this?

4. Write the label quotation next to the quotation from number three above and the word commentary above the student responses. Explain that these are examples of what the group will be doing.

5. Distribute the Character Chart Advance Organizer (Attachment 1, page 77).

6. Direct the students to look at number 1. "The author comments directly on the character." The students fill in the quotation and commentary in the space provided.

7. Examine the other questions with the students and then, according to the maturity of the students, complete the chart as a

class or group activity.

8. Inform students that this is the raw material for writing a character analysis essay.

9. Review the elements of an informative/persuasive essay. Students may write a four or five paragraph essay that includes introductory and concluding paragraphs.

A possible paragraph organization is as follows:

— Introduction in which students state the intention of demonstrating and evaluating the author's portrayal of the character.

— Using the quotations and commentary from questions 1, 2, and 3 of the character chart, students write a paragraph that dis-

cusses both the author's description of and direct comments on the character.

— Using the quotation and commentary from question 5, students write a paragraph on how the other characters react to the old fairy or her actions. (Number 4 would be included if applicable.)

— Using the quotation and commentary from question 6, students write a paragraph on what the character actually says.

— In the concluding paragraph, students will summarize how this character is presented and evaluate the degree to which the author treats the character fairly.

Closure

Students peer edit each others' essays, complete a second draft, and share their final drafts in groups or with the class.

Extensions

Individual students choose another fairy tale and then complete a character commentary on a chosen character.

If students conclude the character was not treated fairly, they may rewrite the story presenting an alternative view.

Create an illustrated character quotation book using appropriate quotations, commentaries or both developed in this unit.

Assessment

Students and teachers may assess the essay according to the rubrics similar to those used for TAKS writing.

Notes

Attachment 1
Character Chart

After selecting a character, use the following to create your own character charts. You will need a minimum of three quotes for each section.

1. What the character says:

Page No.	Quote	Commentary

2. What the other characters say to the character:

Page No.	Quote	Commentary

3. What other characters say about the character:

Page No.	Quote	Commentary

4. The author shows the actions of the character:

Page No.	Quote	Commentary

5. The author describes character's physical appearance:

Page No.	Quote	Commentary

6. The author comments directly on the character:

Page No.	Quote	Commentary

Unit 10
Boldly Going Where
We've Not Gone Before

Areas of Giftedness
- Creative Thinking
- Fine Arts
- General Intellectual Ability
- Leadership
- Specific Academic Areas
  - Language Arts
  - Science
  - Social Studies

Grade Levels
4–6

Duration
6 weeks

Generalizations
- Adventures require risk-taking and sacrifice.
- Adventures originate from a variety of motives.
- Adventures can be found while exploring the past, present, and future.
- Adventures create opportunities for discovery.
- Adventures result in growth and change.

Theme:
Explorations

Grade Levels:
4–6

Developer:
Susan Lucenay

Objective	Activities	Interdisciplinary Connections
• Students will demonstrate knowledge of the motives and risks undertaken by adventurers. See Lesson Plan 1, Page 82	• List attributes of characters from movie clips. • Name historical and present day adventurers with these attributes. • Interview adults to determine how many "followed their dreams." Create a class book with the results. • Determine motives, risks, and sacrifices of adventures. • Design motivating poems, posters, etc., to inspire others to "catch" the spirit of adventure.	• Social Studies, Reading, Language Arts • Language Arts, Social Studies • Social Studies, Language Arts, Fine Arts
• Students will use what they learn about adventurers and apply it in a study of early explorers. See Lesson Plan 2, Page 84	• Read excerpts from journals of adventurers. • Convince Congress to finance a plan for space or world exploration. • Debate the wise use of the funds. • Simulate the cramped quarters of ships by putting large boxes together to work in for a while. • Design a game to play while in the cramped area by yourself to ease the boredom sometimes encountered on long journeys. • Research a "New World" explorer in small groups. Present data discovered to class as the obituary of the explorer or as a news report/ interview. Design posters or travel brochures. • Develop a timeline of the explorers and their accomplishments.	• Reading, Social Studies, Science, Math • Social Studies, Science, Math • Social Studies, Creative Thinking, • Social Studies, Fine Arts, Creative Thinking • Social Studies, Reading, Language Arts • Social Studies
• Students will demonstrate what they have learned about explorers and the cultures they encountered by creating a culture and designing artifacts to reflect that culture. See Lesson Plan 3, Page 86	• Students will analyze common items in our culture to determine values and other universals listed on an outline. • Compare cultures within our country, state, city, and classroom. • Create a culture in a small group and develop artifacts that represent it. • Groups exchange artifacts and try to determine culture. Complete outline. • Look at labels in clothes in closets and determine where the clothes came from.	• Social Studies, Reading, Language Arts
• Students will explore the Mayan culture to determine the importance of trade and cooperation to a culture's success. See Lesson Plan 4, Page 88	• Investigate the Mayan culture and complete the culture outline (see Attachment 3, page 89). • Search the Maya Quest reports to learn more about the economy.	• Reading, Social Studies, Language Arts

Authentic Methods and Context	Resources	Assessment
• Throughout the year, read about contemporary adventurers in science, business, etc. Keep a notebook or bulletin board as a record of their accomplishments.	• Clips from television or movies, "We Are All Explorers," poem. (See Attachment 1, page 84.)	• Teacher and student-designed rubrics incorporating criteria assessing student-made products.
• Plan a trip and determine how much it costs to buy supplies. • Investigate methods of navigation and log keeping.	• http://gorp.away.com	
• Design a system of organization to use at your desk to keep things close. • Design a game to play in the car by yourself or with a friend.	• List of "Sailor's Superstitions" (see Attachment 2, page 86). • Columbus, C. (1990). *I, Columbus.* New York: Walker & Co. • Conrad, P. (1991). *Pedro's journal.* Honesdale, PA: Caroline House. • Moulton, G. (Ed.). (2002) *The definitive journals of Lewis and Clark.* Lincoln, NE: University of Nebraska Press. • http://www.jasonproject.org • Dig II simulation, Interact, see: www.interact-simulations.com.	• Student and teacher-selected criteria will be used to develop rubrics to evaluate games, presentations, and journals.
• Write your own obituary that you would like to see many years from now showing all of your accomplishments.		
• Develop a timeline of your own life projecting it over the next 75 years.		
• Investigate the Archaeological Conservancy Organization to identify the sites closest to your home. Find out what can be done to preserve sites.	• Outline of Culture Universals (see Attachment 3, page 89).	• Student and teacher-selected criteria will be used to develop rubrics to assess the design of the culture and the authenticity of the items chosen to represent the universals. • Another rubric can be developed to assess the findings of the "Dig" and the accuracy of the conclusions.
• Ask a grocer from which country certain produce originates. Identify this country on a map. Draw conclusion as to the relationship between location and economy.		

Objective	Activities	Interdisciplinary Connections
	• Complete the culture and universal outline as a class or as a small group.	• Social Studies, Reading, Language Arts
	• Discuss how the culture began as one in economic subsistence level and evolved to one of wealth.	• Social Studies
	• Determine the dates of the Spanish invasion and the dates of the beginning of the fall of the Mayan Empire.	
	• Design a mural telling the story and using the artistic methods of Mayan artisans.	• Fine Arts
	• Build models of Mayan pyramids.	• Social Studies, Fine Arts

"Discovery consists of seeing what everybody has seen

Lesson Plan 1

Boldly Going Where We've Not Gone Before
Adventurers

Lesson Objectives

Students will study adventurers, their motives and the sacrifices often demanded of these risk-takers, in order to understand the "Spirit of Adventure."

Prerequisite Skills

None.

Materials

Books, comic books, movie clips of adventurers, miscellaneous materials for student-made products.

Introduction

Show students various film clips, such as *Field of Dreams*, *Back to the Future*, one of the *Indiana Jones* movies, or *The Spirit of St. Louis*, which depict various adventurous characters. Clips might also be shown from television shows such as *Star Trek*, *The Cape*, *Promised Land*, *The Adventures of Robin Hood*, *Little House on the Prairie*, and *Early Edition* or any of the action-packed cartoons shown these days. (Use examples from books if video clips are not available.)

Activity Descriptions

1. Have students list adjectives on the board that describe the adventurous characters in the film clips. Try to come up with at least 10 attributes that most characters share (e.g., risk-taker, weird, courageous, caring, curious).

2. Have students name other people from history that shared some of the characteristics of these adventurers and what they discovered or strived for. Students may also want to list other characters from novels, cartoons, television shows, movies, and so forth, that have these characteristics (especially if their knowledge of history is limited).

3. Make a list of contemporary people who would be considered adventurers, explorers, or risk-takers and what the spirit of adventure is motivating them to achieve. What real-life adventurers do students know personally?

4. Are we losing the spirit of adventure, the quest for discoveries, or inventive-

Authentic Methods and Context	Resources	Assessment

- Using only limited money, work out a budget for a new business and determine how long it would take to begin making a profit.

- Determine how many parents make a living providing services or products. Discover how the class's families are economically interdependent on each other.

- Internet sites:
  http://gorp.away.com
  http://www.earthwatch.org

- Students will prepare rubrics with teacher and student-selected criteria to assess presentations of findings about cultures.
- Teacher observations will be used to discern whether or not students feel comfortable using economic terminology.

and thinking what nobody has thought."

ness in America? Discuss.

5. Ask students to interview several adults to determine if they were able to pursue their childhood dreams. Why or why not? Have students make an illustrated page for each adult surveyed: "I wanted to be a _____, instead I became a _____." Put pages together to form a classroom book.

6. What are some of the hazards or risks that some explorers or adventurers endure? Give specific examples of things that happened to specific adventurers. Was it worth the price they had to pay?

7. Discuss: Risk-takers are often viewed as weird or just plain crazy. Why is that? Do you agree? Give examples. What if all

"adventurers" were allowed to go live in a space station in outer space. How might that affect those left on Earth? What if there were no risk-takers in our society? Discuss.

8. What motivates adventurers? Have students list several of their ideas on the board. Early explorers were often motivated by the three "G's" … God, glory, and gold. How many of the students' ideas could be put into these three categories? Are there other reasons for taking risks?

Closure

Read the poem, "We Are All Explorers" from Attachment 1 on page 84. Students will design motivating posters, artwork, games, ban-

ners, or write poetry that inspire other students to catch the "Spirit of Adventure" and to hang on to their dreams, pursue their goals, and so forth.

Some students may want to imagine that they were the architect of a new school and decide how they would design it to encourage students toward being adventurers.

Discuss various contemporary slogans such as Nike's "Just Do It" and encourage students to come up with an original slogan or phrase.

Extension

Throughout the year, students can look for examples in newspapers and magazines of people who have taken a risk and attempted to "go boldly where they have not gone before." An example would be the Texas woman who wanted to duplicate (successfully this time) Amelia Earhart's attempt to fly around the world. Introduce the term *entrepreneur* and have students look for examples of risk-taking in the business field. Space exploration is a popular area for exploration. Researchers in any field often publish their findings and students can bring examples to share. These modern examples of the "spirit of adventure" may be assembled into a bulletin board that is continually updated throughout the year.

Assessment

Student-designed rubrics would be submitted as students design their project. They should reflect the theme of the "spirit of adventure" and be motivational, attractive, and have other student-selected criteria.

Attachment 1

We Are All Explorers

We are all explorers.
Even those of us who seldom leave home
Are forever making journeys of discovery
As we come across something new.

Our emergence from the womb, our first crawl,

Our first friendship, our first job,
Are all acts of exploration; and since human beings
Have been indulging in these activities
Since the beginning of time, it follows that
The instinct to explore is a characteristic
As old as the race itself.

Curiosity is a basic human trait.
We all want to know what lies behind
A locked door or a mischievous smile.
Equally basic is the wish to find a better
Hunting ground, or a better job,
Or, why the neighbor's grass is greener than ours.
Such basic motives have been enough to account
For mankind's exploration of the Earth.

This wish to acquire knowledge has,
In the last thousand years, been the motive behind most of the truly great feats of exploration.
Lust of knowing is not, however,
The only attribute explorers have needed.
They have frequently needed great powers of endurance,
And have always needed courage.

Why?

Echoing the words of John F. Kennedy,
"Not because it's easy—but because it's hard."

Human adventure, quest, and achievement
Comes from those individuals who want to know more
For the good of mankind.

Lesson Plan 2

Boldly Going Where We've Not Gone Before
Adventurers

Lesson Objectives

Students will use what they learned about adventurers and apply it to a study of early explorers of the New World.

Prerequisites

Students should be able to locate the oceans and continents on a map or globe, and realize that adventurers have motives and endure risks, hardships, and sacrifice.

Materials

A globe, a variety of world maps, books, videos, or Internet access to find information on the New World explorers. Measuring tapes (long), large cardboard boxes.

Introduction

Teacher will read to the class the list of sailor's superstitions (Attachment 2, page 86) that were held by some sailors and explorers during the 1400–1500s. Reading this might dramatically create some of the same feelings of concern held by the naive and uneducated sailors.

Activity Descriptions

1. Following a brief background explanation of the importance of Marco Polo's travels to the east and his recording of his findings, students will be given opportunities to read about Christopher Columbus' adventures through primary and secondary sources. Excerpts from his journals are interesting and the novelization of them found in *I, Columbus,* make easy reading. *Pedro's Journal* is another novel that offers interesting insight into this historical journey from the viewpoint of Columbus' cabin boy. *National Geographic* has several issues that show the latest research into the discoveries claimed by Columbus. As a class, discuss Columbus' motives, the risks, hardships, and sacrifices involved with his adventures.

2. Columbus had to convince Ferdinand and Isabella to finance the voyage. Read about his efforts. Have students decide how to convince

Congress to plan for space exploration. Students can use a debate format to give reasons for it and reasons to oppose it. Is there a better use for the money, or can the expense be justified?

3. Explorers keep careful observations and record their data in their journals. Often diagrams are drawn to illustrate what they see when words are inadequate. Students are to "choose their own adventure" and find a place to explore that they have not seen before. This can be a part of the school or the school grounds, a neighbor's yard, a park, or anything else that comes to mind. They will plan how they will explore it and how they will document their findings. Reading selections from the journals of Lewis and Clark also give excellent examples of descriptive journal writings that were frequently illustrated. (Students may need to review how to measure area (length x width) and decide how accurate they should be in their measurements. Measuring the length of their own feet or their natural "stride" can be helpful in estimation, or they may want to use a measuring tape.) Students will finally need to decide

how they will report their findings to their class. Was the class able to visualize the area from the description in the journal? Have the class attempt to draw pictures simply from listening to the description.

4. Assign 2–3 students a particular New World explorer to research who followed his "spirit of adventure" and went "where no (known) man had gone before." These might include Balboa, Magellan, Cortez, Pizarro, Drake, Hudson, Cabot, Ponce de Leon, Jolliet and Marquette, and DeSoto. Student researchers will need to find out who these men were, what they were looking for, what they found, what the significance of their discovery is, and anything else that they can find out that makes these men unique. Discuss the motives, the hardships, risks, and sacrifices of the explorers.

Closure

Research data should be shared with the class. Examples could be done by writing these explorers' obituaries (after reading examples from the newspapers), or by having the students come to class in costumes and be "interviewed" by news reporters.

Visuals such as posters or travel brochures aid in the

presentation. Another way to present data is having each group create an "Explorer's Notebook" about their explorer's journey. It could include an advertisement to recruit crew members, a "news" article to publicize the impending journey, a map showing the route taken, data about the crew, the ship and hazards met, and documentation of the area "explored." A final report to the king of your accomplishments could also be included.

A classroom timeline can be developed as the various explorers are presented through the student projects.

Extensions

Create an "Explorers" game with a game board and pieces simulating the explorers' adventures. Risk cards might be drawn to simulate hazards that they encounter, and other cards might be drawn to earn "favorable winds," and so forth. Students can design their games in groups and then have a "game day" to play each other's games.

Planning an expedition involves an extreme amount of careful planning. What would the explorer that you research need to take with him on his adventure? If he had known how the trip would turn out, would he have equipped his ship differently? How much would it cost to equip a ship with these items today?

Students may wish to eval-

uate each explorer by giving him a "report card" on which several criteria are listed such as leadership skills, organization, perseverance, community relations, ethical conduct, and so forth. The men are graded, and justification for giving that grade must be detailed on the report card using specific facts and examples.

Explorers used several different methods of navigation such as using the stars through the navigational instruments developed at that time. Research these methods. How do airplanes and ships navigate today? Explore the use of the 360° compass and the quadrant system. How does radar work? What part do satellites play in navigation today?

Assessment

Student-designed rubrics can be developed for the explorer presentations and the explorer games.

Attachment 2

Sailor's Superstitions

1. Sailing from port on Friday dooms the voyage.
2. Only the foolish sail too far from home, for they may become caught in currents of extreme strength and be pulled off of the edge of the world.
3. Beware of sea serpents, for they can tip over the

unwary ship with their tails.
4. Watch that the ship doesn't list starboard while in port ... for that is a warning of an upcoming voyage of danger.
5. If a person sneezes while on your left, the voyage is doomed.
6. If a goblin is sighted, sail away quickly for they can tear your sails and snarl your lines.
7. Never cut your hair or your fingernails in fair weather while at sea or you will be cutting through stormy weather soon.
8. It is a sign of warning if you find knives crossed at the table ... beware!
9. Spilling salt will surely lead to bad luck.
10. Keep a sharp lookout for giant whirlpools found at sea. They will pull in ships of any size and never be seen again.

Lesson Plan 3

Boldly Going Where We've Not Gone Before
Cultures

Lesson Objectives

Students will demonstrate what they have learned about explorers and the cultures they encountered by creating a culture, and designing artifacts to reflect that culture.

Prerequisites

Students should have a general understanding about the U.S. government and economy.

Materials

Culture universal outline; miscellaneous materials with which to make artifacts; dirt field or dirt-filled aquarium, shovels, spoons, toothbrushes for "dig" (optional); pictures from current magazines.

Introduction

Students will be introduced to the concepts of a culture and the culture universals found on an outline. Contemporary items (or pictures of items in current magazines) will be examined to see how they reflect our culture today. Discuss:

1. What things are important, or have great value, in today's culture? Give examples of how they are reflected in various universals such as the clothing, modes of transportation, and so forth.

2. What items of today best reflect our culture? How could these be misinterpreted if discovered as artifacts years from now by future cultures?

3. What part of our culture would be hard to interpret with artifacts? Complete the Culture Universal Outline (see Attachment 3, page 89) together as a group activity describing the culture of our hometown.

Activity Descriptions

1. As a class, discuss differences that they are aware of between our culture and cultures currently found in other countries. Ask: What cultural differences did the European explorers encounter when they arrived in the New World? Also, it might be interesting to discover differences in cultures found within our state and within our own city. Are there differences within our school? Within our classroom?

2. Introduce basic archaeological steps to be followed when artifacts are unearthed in digs.

3. Divide students into two groups. Each group is challenged to create an original culture from the past and design artifacts which represent that culture. They should draw or take pictures of these artifacts and write down what that item represents in the culture.

4. If possible, each team will "bury" the artifacts (possibly even breaking the artifacts into pieces). The "oldest" artifact would be buried the deepest, and the most recent artifacts would be found near the surface. If no dirt field or aquarium is available, the artifacts may simply be traded, as if they have just been found. Data cards may indicate where they were found.

5. The groups trade sides and now are in the discovery stage. Using careful archaeological methods, the students dig up the artifacts and record where they found them.

6. The teams look at all of the artifacts and data and complete a culture universal outline based on what they predict the culture was like.

Closure

Students share their findings and predictions with the other team. The creating team presents their original culture for comparison. Teams discuss accuracy, validity of conclusions drawn, and interpretations made from artifacts.

Extensions

Using what they have learned about this imaginary culture, students can create an adventure story whose setting is in this strange culture. Students can also imagine a culture of the future or one that has been discovered on another planet.

Investigate the archaeological conservancy. Locate archaeological sites close to your home.

Assessment

Students will design a rubric using teacher and student-selected criteria to use in the assessment of the design of their culture and the authenticity of the items chosen to represent the various universals. Rubrics can also be designed based on the findings of the "dig" and the accuracy of their conclusions.

Adapted from *DIG II* simulation, by Interact.

Lesson Plan 4

Boldly Going Where We've Not Gone Before
Mayan Culture

Lesson Objectives

Students will explore the Mayan culture to determine the importance of trade and cooperation to a culture's success.

Prerequisites

Understanding what makes up a culture.

Materials

Map of Mexico; pictures of the Mayan people, Mayan ruins, and artifacts; Culture Universal Outline (see Attachment 3, opposite page); butcher paper; computer and access to the Internet (optional).

Introduction

Introduce the economic concepts of subsistence level, specialization by product and service, surplus, and interdependence. A video series is available through the Joint Council of Economic Education and Baylor University Economic Education Department.

Activity Descriptions

1. On a map of the Mexican Yucatán, locate the main cities in which the Mayan civilization flourished. Show pictures of various ruins, murals, and artifacts that were found.
2. Use "Maya Quest" interactive Internet report of various scientists as they explore the Mayan ruins and the mysteries that permeate them. Observe the lifestyle of the modern Mayan people.
3. Discuss how a civilization goes from one that just gets by (is on the subsistence level), to one that gradually has people that begin to specialize either by providing a service or by producing a product and developing a surplus. Determine products that were produced at various sites that were surplus and were traded with other Mayan cities. How can we determine that this civilization was beyond the subsistence level? (They had time to make items that were simply for beauty. They had time for fun.) What modes of transportation were used in trading?
4. Complete Culture Universal Outline (see Attachment 3, page 89) together on the Maya using books, videos, or the computer to locate information as a class project or divide the class into small groups and assign parts of the outline to the groups.
5. Discuss how the invasion of the Spanish affected the productivity of the culture by cutting off trade routes and isolating various cities. The cities had been interdependent on one another.
6. Students may want to build models of Mayan pyramids, study their calendar and other artifacts, and read about the myths of the culture.

Closure

Divide students into three groups. Each group designs a mural showing the development of the Mayan culture and its demise after the invasion of the Spanish.

Extension

Students will determine various products that are produced only in certain states for which we in Texas trade our surplus. What surplus products or services do we as a country trade with other countries? What would happen if some of this trade was discontinued? How can the geography, climate, or environment affect the economic development of a country?

Students may go through their closet and make a list of the clothing items and where each one was made. They may also want to go to the grocery store and ask the produce manager where the various produce items originate.

Students may want to study other interesting cultures such as the Aztec, the Inca, and the Anasazi, to determine the strength of their economies and to determine the cause(s) of the declines in their cultures. Culture Universal Outlines (see Attachment 3, this page) can be completed on these cultures.

Assessment

Student-designed rubrics can be used to assess the murals. Teacher observation can be used to determine whether students are able to identify the economic features of the culture and understand the cause and effect of various outside forces on a culture's economy.

Attachment 3

Culture Universal Outline

I. **Culture Background**
   A. Time culture exists
   B. Geographic setting
   C. Physical characteristics of people

II. **Themes**
   A. Values: What is important to the culture?
   B. Ethics: What is right or wrong within this culture?
   C. Symbols: What is a symbol of importance within the culture?

III. **Economics**
   A. Technology: What advancements have the people made?
   B. Division of labor: Who does what work?
   C. Trade and money: Describe trade practices. What is used for money?

IV. **Food, Clothing, and Shelter**
   A. Food: How is it produced? What animals are domesticated?
   B. Clothing: Adornment and hairstyles
   C. Shelter and dwellings: Of what are the dwellings made and how are they used?
   D. Types of transportation

V. **Family and Kin**
   A. Marriage and type of family groupings
   B. Child training: Puberty, and rites of passage

VI. **Political Organization**
   A. Government: How is it organized? How are leaders selected?
   B. Conflicts: How are group and individual conflicts resolved?

VII. **Attitude Toward the Unknown**
   A. Religion and religious practices
   B. Death: Beliefs and rituals

VIII. **Communications**
   A. Language: Verbal and written
   B. Number system

IX. **Arts and Aesthetic Values**
   A. Music: Songs and instruments
   B. Artistic forms: What is beautiful to them? How do they depict it?

X. **Recreation**
   A. Games and sports
   B. Use of leisure time: What do they do for fun?

Notes

Unit 11
Governmental Systems

Areas of Giftedness
- Creativity
- General Intellectual Ability
- Leadership

Grade Levels
4–6

Duration
5 weeks (Pullout)

Generalizations
- Crucially important to the success of a democracy is the recognition of people that their input is vitally important.
- Understanding the democratic system empowers citizens to participate effectively.
- In the U.S. democracy, fairness is assured by the constitutional provision for a balance of power.
- The ultimate purpose of the representative democracy is to protect the rights of all people.

**Theme:
Explorations**

**Grade Levels:
4–6**

**Developers:
Dr. Marilyn Rice
and
Lee Lorber**
in collaboration with
Steve Lemons
John Feekin
and Jo Allen

Objective	Activities	Interdisciplinary Connections
• Students will demonstrate increased awareness of *community* in government.	• **Students create a simple acrostic using the word *community*.**	• Social Studies
	• **Teacher gives background information from the article, "The People of the Longhouse."**	• Language Arts
	• **Teacher reads to students, *Many Circles, Many Paths*.**	
• Students will evaluate a situation and discover they can create change within the democratic system.	• **Read a scenario that describes a problem.**	• Social Studies, Language Arts
	• **Students will write a letter to a local representative regarding concerns over the problem in the scenario.**	
• Students will demonstrate understanding of balance of power and participate in group decision-making process. **See Lesson Plan 1, Page 94**	• **See simulation on Lesson Plan 1, page 94, *The Power to Decide*.**	• Social Studies, Language Arts (Math and Science may also be included as students examine the economic and environmental impact of the proposed parking lot.)
• Students will discuss hypothetical situations and determine possible rights and violations **See Lesson Plan 2, Page 99**	• **Week 1: See introduction activity, Lesson Plan 1.** • **Give Bill of Rights handout (see Attachment 6, page 101) to students and apply this document to "the make-believe theft" scenario.**	• Social Studies, Language Arts
	• **Week 2: Group students according to instructions. (See Attachments 7 & 9, pages 102–103, & 104.)** • **Distribute scenarios.** • **Students present their scenarios.** • **Teacher introduces and discusses Kohlberg. (See Attachment 8, page 10.)** • **Teacher uses "Balance of Power" transparency (see Attachment 10, page 105) to show students where the Amendments or Bill of Rights fits.**	

Authentic Methods and Context	Resources	Assessment
• Paula Underwood is an authentic voice of Iroquois history.	• *Jr. Scholastic.* October 21, 1988, pp. 12–14.	• Students conclude lesson by writing a more complex acrostic that demonstrates their growth in under-standing.
	• Underwood, P. (1994). *The native American learning stories.* San Anselmo, CA: A Tribe of Two Press.	
	• Underwood, P. (1994). *Many circles, many paths: A native American learning story.* San Anselmo, CA: A Tribe of Two Press.	
• Write letters to legislators concerning social problems and mail in the most effective products.	• Sydney Parnes' Creative Problem Solving Method (CPS).	• Evaluate letters using a rubric.
• Procedures are practiced that imitate real city council meetings.	• City council meetings.	• Teacher observation of role-playing and deci-sion making (see Attachment 5, page 99).
• Prepare a field trip to a local court house to watch a civil case prosecuted.	• All handouts and material are included in this lesson.	• Student responses to the 3 questions at the end of the lesson will be evaluated as well as student participation in scenarios.

Lesson Plan 1

Governmental Systems
The Power to Decide

Lesson Objectives

By participating in a simulation where the power to make decisions is in the hands of more than one person, students will understand the balance of power and improve their participation in group decision-making.

Prerequisite Skills

Understanding point of view, negotiating, compromise, and self interest.

Materials

Transparencies of the neighborhood map (Attachment 1, page 96), Balance of Power (Attachment 10, page 105). Transparencies and handouts: Roles of Participants (Attachment 3, page 97), Background Information (Attachment 2, page 97), City Council Meeting (Attachment 4, page 98), and rubric: The Power to Decide (Attachment 5, page 99).

Introduction

Suppose you love skateboarding and the city's park department plans to build in an area for skateboarding a nearby park.

Who would you want to plan this? An elderly gentleman whose grandchild just broke his neck skateboarding, the world's skateboarding champion, or a visitor from a foreign country who has never seen rollerskates or a skateboard? None of these would be likely to have a viewpoint that would be adequate. How could the decision be well made? Bring in an expert on the building of a skateboard pad. Also, have persons from the community provide varying points of view.

Activity Description

• *Situation*

The teacher presents the following situation to the class using the transparency, "Game Information." It states:

The McDougals are new immigrants from Scotland. They own and operate a neighborhood grocery store. Next to the store is a large grassy lot with beautiful mature trees. The McDougals have purchased this lot. Whenever weather permits, the neighborhood children play in this park-like area. The McDougals feel the need to expand their store because their two children are nearing college-age and they think they will probably need the money to help pay for this expense. At this time, the land is zoned residential and they want to submit a request to the city council to rezone it commercial so they can use it for the increased parking area they think they will need.

The Patricks live next door.

Their two children especially enjoy the play area. They have recently purchased a croquet set so they can play with their friends. The Johnson children have a net they sometimes put up for neighborhood volleyball and badminton games. In addition, a tire swing and a tree house have been added for the children's use. All of the families living in the area are aware that the increased traffic, noise, and so forth will lower the value of their homes, as well as spoil a favorite neighborhood gathering place and play area.

• *Teacher Strategy*

The teacher will:

1. Hand out Game Information sheets (see Attachments 1 & 2, pages 96–97. Have students review silently.

2. Ask what might be the viewpoints of each homeowner when they first learn about the McDougals' plans. (Perhaps they might respond immediately out of self-interest.) Ask students what might be the viewpoints of the city council at first. (They may be biased toward business or homeowners at first!)

3. Students should be divided into groups (i.e., council members, mayor, city planner, and homeowners). The homeowners should be divided into families (i.e., McDougals,

Patricks, Johnsons, etc.).

4. Ask students to do a PMI on the facts of the game information sheet (Plus, Minus, Interesting analysis developed by Edward de Bono). Students may fold paper vertically in thirds. At the top of the sheet, they may write, "The McDougals' Store." At the top of the three columns they created, they should write +, -, and Interesting. Students should list the positive, negative, and interesting points in the appropriate columns from their character's point of view.

5. Next, students should be divided into groups according to their roles so they can discuss their viewpoints and plan their presentations. See sheets entitled "Roles of Participants (Attachment 3, page 97) and City Council Meeting" (Attachment 4, page 98).

   a) Homeowners divided into families should decide on points they would be negotiable about and that could lead to compromise.

   b) Council members need to understand issues, think through possible alternatives, and the results of these options. The mayor should be primarily a facilitator.

   c) City planner opens meeting and presents information clearly and impartially.

6. Have a council meeting where each side presents what they would like and possible areas of negotiation. Refer to Attachment 4 (page 98), City Council Meeting. (Be sure the map transparency from Attachment 1, page 96, is on the screen.) The city council listens and asks questions. They may or may not come to a conclusion.

Closure

Ask how the power to decide was divided during the simulation. (Teacher may point out that there was a "balance of power.") Ask how the decision would have been made differently if it were made by one person or group. (At this time, guide the students to see that the decisions would reflect a greater degree of self-interest.)

Extensions

Students attend a city council meeting and take notes on what happens. They should note how decisions are made, then share their observations with a family member.

The next class period they should reflect on how their observations portray the concept of "balance of power."

Assessment

Use Rubric "The Power to Decide." (See Attachment 5, page 99.)

Attachment 1
The Power to Decide

In the Zone: Map of the Site

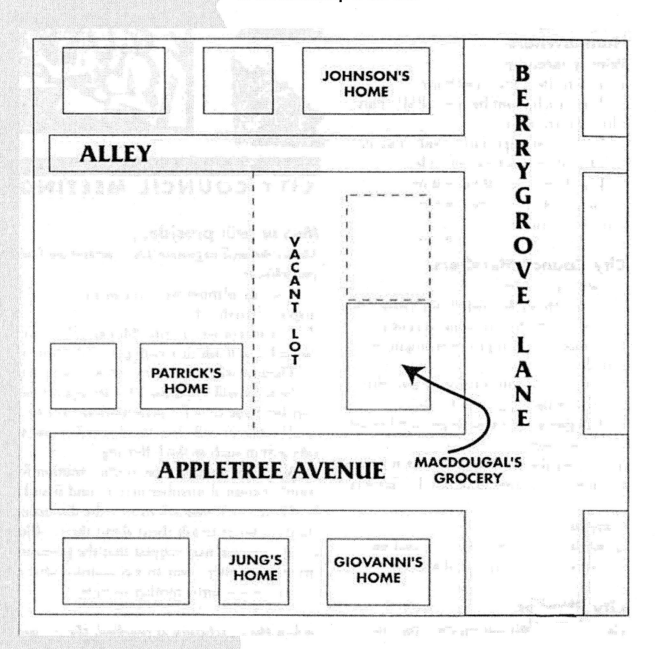

Attachment 2
The Power to Decide

Background Information

The McDougals are new immigrants from Scotland. They own and operate a neighborhood grocery store. Next to the store is a large grassy lot with beautiful mature trees. The McDougals have purchased this lot. Whenever weather permits, the neighborhood children play in this park-like area. The McDougals feel the need to expand their store because their two children are nearing college-age and they think they will probably need the money to help pay for this expense. At this time, the land is zoned residential and they want to submit a request to the city council to rezone it commercial so they can use it for the increased parking area they think they will need.

The Patricks live next door. Their two children especially enjoy the play area. They have recently purchased a croquet set so they can play with their friends. The Johnson children have a net they sometimes put up for neighborhood volleyball and badminton games. In addition, a tire swing and a tree house have been added for the children's use. All of the families living in the area are aware that the increased traffic, noise, and so forth will lower the value of their homes, as well as spoil a favorite neighborhood gathering place and play area.

Attachment 3
The Power to Decide

Roles of Participants

Homeowners

Prior to meeting:
1. Determine viewpoints.
2. Judge each point by using PMI (Plus, Minus, Interesting).
3. Rank most important points. Decide which ones might be negotiable.
4. Plan how you will present or communicate your view points at the council meeting.

City Council Members
1. Study the issues.
2. Think through possible alternatives and what the consequences might be.
3. Think what compromises might be feasible.
4. Think what information you might need from the neighbors and the McDougals so you will be prepared to ask at the meeting.
5. During the meeting, listen carefully and ask questions if necessary for clarification.

Mayor

Lead the city council meeting and see that it runs in an organized fashion.

City Planner

Plan presentation during meeting where the situation is explained in a thorough, professional, and impartial manner.

Attachment 4
The Power to Decide

City Council Meeting • Richardson, Texas

Mayor will preside.
She or he will organize the meeting and assure that the presenters follow the meeting guidelines:

1. The city planner will present the story and issues clearly to the council utilizing the map and overhead.
2. The mayor will ask the McDougals to step forward and present their viewpoint. Note: He will ask that each person give his/her name and address before speaking.
3. Then, he will ask for anyone who supports the request to come forward.
4. Next, he will ask those who are against the request to come forward. (Note: She/he may limit the time for presentations to one or two minutes.)
5. The mayor will close the discussion and will ask for the council to discuss. They may take action such as the following:
   a) A council member may make a motion for or against the McDougals' request. Another council member may second it and the council may vote.
   b) The council may ask during the discussion to have the homeowners come forward for clarification or to ask them about their willingness to accept compromises.
   c) The council may request that the homeowners (including McDougals) try to negotiate so they can come to a conclusion that is mutually satisfying. If so, they will table the discussion until another meeting.

When the conclusion is reached, the mayor will ask for a motion from a council member to close the meeting. She or he will then ask for a second. The council will vote. If a majority agrees the meeting will be concluded.

Attachment 5
Rubric: The Power to Decide

Date: _____

Participant(s): _____ Evaluator(s): _____

Family or Council Member: _____

Name(s): _____

Rank:

Low ————————————————→ High

1. Clarity of presentation	1	2	3	4
2. Understanding of varying viewpoints	1	2	3	4
3. Demonstration of negotiation and compromising skills	1	2	3	4
4. Identification of problem(s)	1	2	3	4
5. Discovery of alternative solutions	1	2	3	4
6. Maintenance of character	1	2	3	4

Total: _____

Comments: _____

Lesson Plan 2

Governmental Systems
Wronged Rights

Lesson Objectives
Students will discuss hypothetical situations and determine possible rights and violations.

Prerequisite Skills
Inferring, analyzing, point of view.

Materials
"Kohlberg Stages" (Attachment 8, page 104) transparency; Amendment Summary sheets (Attachment 6, page 101); "Wronged Rights" (Attachment 7, page 102); "You be the Judge" (Attachment 9, page 104); blank transparencies and pens; "Balance of Power" transparency (Attachment 10, page 105); "Wronged Rights Checklist" (Attachment 11, page 105).

Introduction
Use the following situation to set up the lesson.

Activity Description
* *Situation*

Before the lesson, pick two confident, self-assured girls, preferably a 6th grader and a 4th grader, and talk to them privately. Explain that the older girl will accuse the younger girl in a "make believe" theft. The younger girl will respond to the older girl's demand and empty her purse in front of the class. The older girl will shout something like, "That's my money!" as she retrieves the bill that has been planted in the younger girls purse. Then, the teacher may ask:
* *Focus*
  What would you do if you

were the accused in this scenario?

- *Discussion*
1. Explain your decision or tell why you would react in a certain way.
2. Think of several things you could do. Which one is best?
3. Can anyone help you solve this problem?
4. What will your parents think when they learn you "took" the money?
5. How should you react to unfair actions from others?
6. Were there some rights that were violated? How can we know?
7. We may start by looking at the first 10 amendments to the Constitution called the "Bill of Rights."

This could be a stopping point for the first week of this lesson.

- *Teaching Strategy*

The teacher will:

Remind students that in a previous week's lesson, we looked at the development of our governmental system from a foundation of sense of community. Explain that the Constitution was drafted to unite the 13 original colonies into one nation. Its primary goal was to set up a government with a balance of power so that there could be a democratic system with checks and balances and not a dictatorship or single ruler. Key states in the colonies refused to adopt or ratify the Constitution, however, until the first Congress agreed to adopt a Bill of Rights. explain that these are a shortened, simplified version of the original document. Let students read through the Bill of Rights. Ask

them what rights might have been violated during the "make believe" theft (Amendments 4,6, & 9). Have them explain why they think so.

1. Divide students into 6 groups. Distribute the situations (dilemmas) so that each situation is in the hands of two groups. (See Attachment 7, page 102.)
2. Have students individually read situations and fill in the worksheets "Wronged Rights Checklist" (see Attachment 11, page 105), and "You Be the Judge" (see Attachment 9, page 104). They may move to any part of the room. Suggest that they read the situations two or three times along with the Bill of Rights so they may thoughtfully draw conclusions.
3. Have the small groups then come together and prepare responses to the following questions:

- *Focus*

You are the accused in our situation. What do yo do?

- *Discussion*

Think of several things you could do. Which one is best? Can anyone help you solve the problem?
What will your parents or friends think when they learn of your actions?
How should you react to unfair actions from others?

4. These responses can be summarized on team transparencies and then presented by one team member.
(Reasoning behind decisions must be given at each step.)
5. The teacher may guide the

students to see that the conclusions may vary according to the different interpretations of the students.

6. At the end of the report, the group that had the same situation may give its reactions which may be very different.
7. This will be repeated until all six groups have reported their interpretations.
8. Have the class look at a transparency of the stages of moral development (see Attachment 8, page 104). Discuss these briefly with them.
9. Ask the class to decide where the cafeteria manager belongs in the development stages and why. What about Billy's dad? Why? Roy B. Head? Why? The policeman? Why? (Values clarification is a very sensitive issue in our district so we do not dwell on the moral stages with younger students.)

Closure

1. After the forum, ask how the quote, "Your right to swing your arm ends where my nose begins," applies to this lesson (see Attachment 10, page 105).
2. Refer to the chart, "Balance of Power," and ask where the Bill of Rights fits in. (It assures that the Constitution of the people, or foundation of the government, is guaranteed power through those rights.)
3. Ask students to recall other situations where there may be differing interpretations of individual rights. Why? (Self-

interest, varying experiences, differing skills in observing and thinking as well as different learning styles.)

4. Have students analyze the thinking skills they used in the lesson.

5. Ask what generalizations about systems apply to this lesson. Students may begin to generate some original generalizations about rights as systems.

Extensions

Find an article on violated rights in a local newspaper and discuss the "wronged rights" with a family member.

Assessment

1. What were the most important ideas you learned from this lesson?

2. How might you use this information in your everyday life?

3. Put yourself in the place of a character from one of the scenarios; describe how you would have acted differently and why?

Attachment 6
Bill of Rights

Amendment 1

Guarantees the freedom of religion, speech, the press, and the right to hold peaceful meetings. Gives you the right to ask the government to correct any wrongs against you.

Amendment 2

Gives people the right to own guns.

Amendment 3

Protects you from being forced to feed and house soldiers in your home during peacetime.

Amendment 4

You, your home, or your property can't be searched unfairly.

Amendment 5

Promises that you can't be made to be a witness against yourself or be tried for the same crime twice. You can't be punished without a fair trial. The government can't take your property without paying you fairly.

Amendment 6

Promises you a public trial within a short time in a criminal case. Gives you the right to know what you are charged with, to see and question witnesses against you, and to have a lawyer defend you.

Amendment 7

Gives you the right to be tried by a jury in a private lawsuit.

Amendment 8

Protects you from being given an unreasonable fine or bail, or punished in a cruel or unusual way.

Amendment 9

You have basic rights even though they may not be listed in the Constitution.

Amendment 10

Gives the states or the people all powers that aren't given to the federal government.

Attachment 7

Wronged Rights?
You Be the Judge

1. An Interrupted Lunch

Background

Gloria Lamzusk is a Lootee. It is her second day in America. She lived in the country of Trampole for 13 years before moving to the United States. In Trampole, at exactly 12:15 in the afternoon, all Lootees lie on their backs and loudly chant to their Lootee god. This ritual usually lasts for only a few seconds. It is customary and traditional for all Lootees and, according to past writings, must be done. It is also necessary for Gloria to carry a nonpoisonous snake at all times. It is a symbolic animal used to chase away evil spirits.

Situation

Gloria already made several new friends in America. Things were going great. On the day before she was to start attending her new school, she decided to go shopping at the mall. It contained the largest and most popular cafeteria in town. Gloria had heard many good things about the food and decided to have lunch there. Everything was wonderful—that is, until 12:15 when Gloria, in front of everyone in the cafeteria, fell flat on her back and began her Lootee chant. The cafeteria went silent, and Gloria thought that this silence was in respect to her own Lootee traditions. She finished her chant, returned to her chair, and resumed eating. At this point, everyone pointed and laughed and continued staring at Gloria.

The cafeteria manager brought a policeman, Officer Modsquad, to the scene. He quickly approached Gloria. Gloria felt isolated and threatened. She believed that she could only do one thing at this point. She removed the three foot snake from her purse and began waving it at Officer Modsquad. As she waved the snake, she chanted her Lootee spirit chasing ritual. According to witnesses at the scene, this cleared the cafeteria quickly. Officer Modsquad drew his gun and shot the snake dead. He then handcuffed Gloria and took her to the squad car waiting outside.

What do you think?

2. Mistaken Identity

Background

Mr. Roy B. Head lived in a nice middle-class neighborhood. He had two children, ages 9 and 12. He and his wife both worked, and the house was unoccupied a majority of the week. He was an upstanding citizen who was involved with church and many charities. He was a great guy and wonderful father. Roy and his neighbors were greatly concerned during the past few weeks. Several houses in the neighborhood had been burglarized and the community was quite anxious, as were the police. Roy's house alone had been hit three times in the last month. His insurance company was about to drop him because of all his claims. He was becoming very bitter. The police would come, file a report, and that seemed to be it. Nothing, apparently, was being done. Roy was fit to be tied. He didn't know what to do.

The police were equally frustrated. They had beefed up patrols in the area and were waiting for something to break. They were as tense as the neighborhood was about trying to get this case solved. They had reports of a stranger in the neighborhood. The description of this stranger was a male Caucasian wearing blue jeans, a t-shirt, and beat up tennis shoes.

Situation

It was Tuesday morning and Roy was home alone with a cold. He looked pretty bad. He had not shaven, had on a pair of dirty blue jeans and old t-shirt. He was blowing his nose and reading on the couch when the heard the door knob shake and turn. He was startled at first, but was sure his house was going to get hit by the burglar again. This time it was with him in it. He went and got his hunting shotgun. He looked out the window and did not see anything. He ran to the back of the house and caught a glimpse of a man in a blue shirt. The man looked large and strong. He decided to confront the would-be burglar. At the same time, another man spotted Roy with the gun. He smashed in the door and threw Roy to the floor. He forced his arm back and it accidentally broke. Roy yelled out in pain. Then, there was a strange clanging sound and Roy realized he had been handcuffed. His attackers were the police. He tried to speak, but the police shoved his face into the carpet. Roy was thrown into the back of the squad car. He was not allowed to speak. He tried but the police told him to be quiet.

Roy had no identification and stayed in jail for hours until his wife finally came to report her missing husband.

Were Roy's rights violated? What do you think?

3. Laker Idols

Background

Billy's dad was the biggest Los Angeles Lakers fan that the people of Dallas had ever seen. He would pay as much as $500 for a courtside seat when the Lakers came to town to play the Dallas Mavericks. He admired their coach and idolized their players.

Situation

He even painted his house yellow and purple in honor of the team's colors. Of course, the neighbors complained, but not nearly as loudly as they did when Billy's dad put life-size statues of the starting players around the bird bath in the front yard. A band was hired and so were cheerleaders. Billy's dad knew he often went overboard expressing his love and devotion for his favorite team, but after all, his actions were harmless, and it gave him so much joy.

Bob Clamper, Billy's dad's neighbor, did not view the situation the same way. His house was up for sale for more than a year with little interest.

His real estate agent stated that according to the realtor's analysis, his house and others around Billy's house were greatly depreciating in value while the rest of the neighborhood's homes were rising significantly. The neighborhood homeowners' association was also trying to persuade Billy's dad to act responsibly. They pleaded with Billy's dad to repaint his house. They begged him to put his statues out of sight.

Billy's dad stated that he was not a member of the association and he had no intention of joining the association because the neighborhood was built around his already existing house. He maintained that he has no responsibility or loyalty to that organization.

What do you think? Were any rights violated? Whose?

Attachment 8
Kohlberg's Stages of Moral Development

Stage One
Obey rules to avoid pain or punishment.

Stage Two
Obey rules to obtain rewards or favors.

Stage Three
Follow rules to avoid dislike or disapproval of others.

Stage Four
Obey to avoid punishment by authorities. Legal or religious beliefs govern life.

Stage Five
Major concern is the welfare of the nation or community. Rights of all men put before self.

Stage Six
Conform to self-formulated law.

Attachment 9
You Be the Judge

If you were the judge and you could award up to $1000 for the rights that were violated, how much would you give each victim?

Victim: _____

Amount Awarded: _____

If you could fine (up to $1000) any or all of the characters for demonstrating poor judgment, list the characters and how much you would fine him or her.

Character	Amount Fined	Rationale

Attachment 10
Balance of Power
Checks and Balances

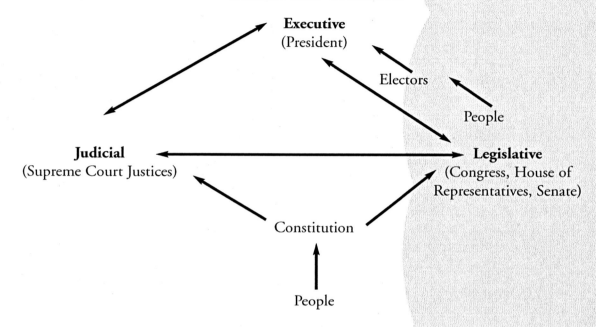

Attachment 11
Wronged Rights Checklist

Characters Victims	Violated Rights Amendment Number	Violation Incident	Violators

Unit 12
It's the Real Thing

Areas of Giftedness
- Creative Thinking
- General Intellectual Ability
- Leadership
- Specific Academic Areas
  - Fine Arts
  - Math
  - Social Studies

Grade Levels
4–6

Duration
8–10 weeks

Generalizations
- Effective language skills are enhanced through advertising.
- Exploring past, present, and future advertising creates universal awareness.
- Universal connections can be made through marketing campaigns.
- Propaganda can be promoted through language and communication.
- Authentic experiences improve problem-solving.

Theme:
Relationships

Grade Levels:
4–6

Developer:
Penny Aklinski

Objective	Activities	Interdisciplinary Connections

Objective

- In their study of advertising, students will use various techniques to create advertising for different media.

See Lesson Plan 1, Page 112

Activities

- **Brainstorm elements of an effective advertisement. Guide students to the five criteria of effective advertisement: see it, read it, understand it, believe it, and want it. Play a prerecorded tape of 10–12 television ads. Discuss whether or not the criteria has been met.**
- **Brainstorm and list familiar advertising slogans. Discuss what makes an effective slogan. Share information to illustrate how slogans have changed through the years.**
- **Design an advertising slogan for school, class, family, and so forth.**
- **Research the history of early advertising.**
- **Compare/contrast old and new magazine ads. Look for changes in values and social attitudes, design, and so forth.**
- **Generate ideas for advertising techniques for the future. Select a product and create two ads that will illustrate a comparison between two time periods. Each should demonstrate a style from either the past, the present, or the future.**
- **Research propaganda techniques (these techniques may be similar but given different names: transfer, bandwagon, testimonial, name calling, repeat, false-image, scientific approach, etc.).**
- **Create a radio advertisement using one of the propaganda techniques and present to the class.**

- **Read the poem, "Clarence" by Shel Silverstein and analyze the influence television commercials have on children and adults. Include infomercials and home shopper advertisements.**
- **Have students create an ad selling the "perfect parents."**
- **Hypothesize how many advertising messages the average person is bombarded with each day (more than 1600). Look around and discover advertising messages within the room (Nike shoes, Apple computers, etc.).**

Interdisciplinary Connections

- Language Arts
- Social Studies
- Social Studies
- Social Studies
- Language Arts, Social Studies
- Technology
- Social Studies
- Science

Authentic Methods and Context	Resources	Assessment
• Visit an advertising agency to see firsthand examples.		• Class discussions and teacher observations.
		• Completed advertising slogan will be evaluated.
		• Completed advertisements will be critiqued using teacher-made rating scale.
• Interview local radio air personalities that read ads for their programs.	• *Grolier's CD-ROM.*	• Group discussion with teacher observations.
	• Mitchell, M. (1970). *Propaganda, polls, & public opinion.* Englewood Cliffs, NJ: Prentice-Hall.	• Completed radio advertisement will be evaluated according to to class-created criteria chart.
• Contact home shopper show to determine criteria used for selecting merchandise.	• Silverstein, S. (1981). *Light in the attic.* New York: Harper & Row.	

Objective	Activities	Interdisciplinary Connections
	• Using the World Almanac (Arts & Media), research to discover how much money the top 100 leading U.S. advertisers spend on advertising in a year. Select three different advertisers and calculate the percentage of monies spent in a given year.	• Social Studies, Math
	• Present findings in a visual representation such as a chart or graph.	
	• Obtain a copy of the classified ads from a newspaper and calculate the cost for selected ads. Design a classified ad and calculate the expense.	• Math
	• Examine the effect of logos on consumers (discuss what makes a logo effective and the use of icons in advertising.) Also, discuss the phenomenon of a brand name becoming the commonly accepted name for a product (i.e., Kleenex, Coke, Ziploc bags, etc.). Brainstorm more examples with students.	• Language Arts
	• Students work in groups to create a logo for a fictitious company and develop their own personal logo.	• Art
• Through a taste test, the students will analyze and connect marketing strategies to effectively sell a product.	• Test and rank four brands of peanut butter in four categories such as: additives, spreadability, texture, and taste (see Attachment 4, page 117). Evaluate the taste test results and its effect in advertising. Create a chart or graph of the results.	• Science, Math
	• Write the company of the winning brand, telling about the test and the results.	• Language Arts
	• Test and rank three brands of soft drinks: Pepsi, Coca-Cola, and a store brand according to taste. Graph results. (see Attachment 5, page 118). Write the winning company and send the results.	• Math
• By applying what they've learned, students will develop and conduct an effective marketing and advertising campaign for a new soft drink.	• Design a marketing campaign to sell a new soft drink.	• Language Arts, Math, Technology
	• Produce a new soft drink. Use club soda as the base and add extracts, kool-aid, and sweeteners.	
	• Develop and create a name, logo, and a slogan. Design a billboard, can cover, and product package.	
	• Design a new television commercial for the new soft drink. Research the steps in producing a TV commercial: write script, do storyboard, film, edit, add sound/special effects, and rehearse. The script and storyboard can be done as a paper and pencil activity, or it may be done using HyperStudio on the computer.	• Language Arts
	• Compete in a class and/or interschool soda competition for the most effective overall campaign.	

Authentic Methods and Context	Resources	Assessment
	• *World Almanac (Arts & Media).*	• Presentation chart graph will be self-evaluated through a performance reflection log.
• Invite the local newspaper to send a resource person to talk about advertising in their newspaper.	• City newspaper.	
	• Addresses of peanut butter companies.	
• Contact the store associated with the store brand of cola. Set up an interview by phone or in person to ask pertinent questions.	• Addresses of cola companies.	
• Visit the Dr. Pepper Museum in Waco, TX, or another bottling company to learn more about the development of a soft drink.	• Sylvester, D. (1986). *Advertising, communication, economics.* The Learning Works, Inc.	
• Visit a billboard company and see first-hand the actual design and making of a highway billboard.		• Student advertising campaign will be critiqued using a teacher-made evaluation form that incorporates student-selected criteria in a rating scale.

Lesson Plan 1

It's the Real Thing
Marketing and Advertising

Lesson Objectives
By applying what they've learned, students will develop and conduct an effective marketing and advertising campaign for a new soft drink.

Prerequisite Skills
Understanding of the five criteria of an effective advertisement.

Materials
VCR, previously-taped commercial and paper materials.

Introduction
Show a video clip of a commercial that has a familiar slogan (i.e., McDonald's, Coca-Cola, etc.).

Activity Description
1. Brainstorm and list familiar slogans with students.
2. Have students try to identify slogans on Attachment 1, page 113. This can be sent home to encourage parent involvement as some of the slogans are outdated for students, but may not be for adults. Challenge students to add slogans they see on television.
3. Discuss what makes an effective slogan.
4. Share information on Attachments 2 and 3 (pages 113 & 114) to illustrate how slogans have changed through the years.
5. Have students design an advertising slogan for their school, class, family, and so forth.

Closure
Students share, discuss, and evaluate their slogan. Compare and contrast actual slogans for effectiveness.

Extensions
Students may extend this by selecting a particular product and looking for past and present slogans to compare and contrast.

To further extend, students may create a slogan for a product in the future. This can be an existing product or a created product.

Assessment
Student's slogan will be critiqued for effectiveness and originality.

Attachment 1
Remember These?
The Power of Advertising

1. Plop, plop, fizz, fizz...
2. Tastes like that good old fashioned lemonade...
3. The breakfast of champions.
4. Reach out, reach out, and touch someone.
5. Please! Don't squeeze the ...
6. Mmmm, Mmmm, Good!
7. Double your pleasure, double your fun ...
8. Don't leave home without it.
9. Get a piece of the rock.
10. The good hands people.
11. Tough enough to overstuff.
12. Dessert isn't dessert without ...
13. It's Grrrrrrreat!
14. The place with the helpful hardware man!
15. It sticks to the skin, not the sore.
16. Sometimes you feel like a nut, sometimes you don't.
17. Snap, crackle, pop!
18. The Uncola!
19. I'm a pepper, he's a pepper.
20. It melts in your mouth, not in your hands.
21. Fly the friendly skies of ...
22. The copper-top battery.
23. It's the mountain grown coffee.
24. We do chicken right!
25. Where's the beef?

Attachment 2
Coca-Cola Over the Years

1886 Drink Coca-Cola.
1904 Delicious and refreshing...
1905 Coca Cola revives and sustains.
1906 The Great National Temperance Beverage...
1917 Three million a day.
1922 Thirst knows no season.
1926 Six million a day.
1927 Around the corner from everywhere.
1929 The pause that refreshes...
1932 Ice-cold sunshine.
1933 The best friend thirst ever had...
1938 Coca-Cola goes along...
1939 Wherever you are, whatever you do, wherever you may be when you think of refreshment, think of ice-cold Coca-Cola.
1942 The only thing like Coca-Cola is Coca-Cola itself. It's the real thing.
1946 Where there's Coke, there's hospitality.
1949 Coca-Cola ... along the highway to anywhere.
1952 What you want is a Coke.
1956 Coca-Cola makes good things taste better.
1957 Sign up good taste.
1958 The cold, crisp taste of Coke...
1959 Be really refreshed.
1963 Things go better with Coke.
1970 It's the real thing.
1971 I'd like to buy the world a Coke.
1975 Look up, America.
1976 Coke adds life!
1979 Have a Coke and a smile.
1982 Coke is it!
1986 Red, White, and You!
1992 You Can't Beat the Real Thing.
1996 Always Coca-Cola.

Attachment 3
Coke is It!

by Charles Madrigan
excerpted from the *Chicago Tribune Service*

Deep inside the corporate headquarters of one of the most enduring symbols of capitalism, the demographers and pollsters and media trolls were hard at work, taking the pulse of America and picking up every little glitch and pattern and changing mood.

This assessment is an ongoing process in the big, brown building downtown, a constant check on what people say and do and think. It is the stuff that business success is made to identify your market. Know your market. Sell your market.

They were watching our national malaise to pick up signs that this bumbling giant of a nation was groping its way toward yet another of its periodic transformations. They had seen it all before. They knew what to watch.

The hostages came home from Tehran, signaling the end of one international headache. Ronald Reagan became President, sending important mood messages into the computers. The moral majority became a serious political force.

The nation salivated over a royal wedding overseas. People started reproducing a good sign for business. There was a

Ninety-five million times a day, Americans pop the top from one of those distinctive bottles ... that is 22 million times more than any other soft drink.

resurgence in the practice of marriage. Even liberals talked about the need for budget control. Our Navy wasted some Libyan jets, just to show it could be done.

And the thinkers in the big, brown building with those glowing red letters across the top watched it all. They measured it. They picked at it. They thought about it. They dined on it. They slept on it. And they spent lots of money on it.

The conclusion: It's time for a change.

If you don't believe that, finish this jingle: "things go better with ..."

That's right, Coke. Coca-Cola. Trademark Registered. It's the Real Thing! I'd Like to Buy the World a Coke! Look Up, America! Coke Adds Life! Have a Coke and a Smile!

And now: Coke Is It!

What?

It's the real thing. The sign of good taste. The cold, crisp taste. What you want is a Coke. The best friend thirst ever had! Buy me. Drink me. Wouldn't you trade your soul for one right now?

Coca-Cola has decided it's time for a new slogan. Actually, time for a whole new campaign. The company has concluded we no longer are a country of self-doubting wimps.

We are a can-do county that has gone far beyond the

1979 slogan, Have a Coke and a Smile.

We are a "Coke Is It" country, and we'll punch you right in the nose if you disagree.

Ninety-five million times a day, Americans pop the top from one of those distinctive bottles or crack a practical red and white can or suck Coke through a straw at a restaurant. That is 22 million times more than any other soft drink.

And when those thinkers in the Atlanta headquarters tell you that the country will soon be tapping its collective toe to "Coke Is It," you can take it to the bank.

Sergio Zyman says it's a sure thing. He is Coca-Cola's vice president for marketing operations in the United States. He was the man who decided we have moved from a "Have a Coke and a Smile" mode into this new "Coke Is It" era. Coca-Cola, he said in a hurried telephone interview that preceded a jet hop to Mexico city, needed something new.

Zyman is a 90-mile-per-hour talker. He reaches this velocity after only a few words. "I think the country is trying to assert itself again," he said. "I think the country is a lot more aggressive than it was in the past."

"It is standing up and being counted, both as individuals and as a nation. We want to tell it like it is. People want to hear it like it is. We're telling the world we are what we are and we are proud of it. You can see the change every place, just every place. So we feel we can say, 'OK, Coke is it!' the most refreshing taste around, the one that never lets you down."

Those slogans, those campaigns, are not born overnight. Nothing is done on the cheap. The commercials must drip mood and sentiment.

Just look at all of those happy television people in previous Coke ads. You never see them drinking Coke at a funeral or an auto accident.

They are always doing American dream things. Picnics play a big role in Coca-Cola advertising and family reunions, too. You get beautiful people singing about unusual foreign aid proposals (I'd Like to Buy the World a Coke). Or, absolutely precious little urchins who swap a Coke for Mean Joe Greene's sweaty jersey.

These are astute, escapist, fantasy ads. They are also wonderful. Who wouldn't want to spend some change to join such a world?

The last thing a company like Coke wants is for these fantasies to become dusty. First thing you know, people will be saying, "Oh sure, Have a Coke and a Smile (yawn). Hey look, over here, the Pepsi Generation is nuking Iran. Gimme some!"

The public is fickle. Were it more stable, Coca-Cola would be able to say, "Drink Coca-Cola" and let it go at that. As a matter of fact, that's how this whole thing started. It was way back in 1886 and Coke was beginning to get a toehold on the south.

"Drink Coca-Cola," its advertising said.

This was the great, great, great-granddaddy of "Coke Is It!"

In 1906, the company realized that fierce bands of moralists were marching around busting up bars with their hatchets. In an astute advertising move, Coca-Cola became "The Great National Temperance Beverage."

By 1939, Coca-Cola ads appeared as though they could have been lifted from the Baltimore Catechism: "Wherever you are, whatever you do, wherever you may be, when you think of refreshment, think of ice-cold Coca-Cola."

It was long, but cosmic.

"The element that links all of these slogans and campaigns," Zyman said, "is that they were all products of their times."

People relate to their times and to their dreams.

You could say, "Here, drink this stuff."

It's much better to say, albeit subliminally, "Drink this stuff and Joe Greene will toss his sweaty shirt at you and you can be at a family reunion and you can send best wishes to the rest of the world, and gawd, life is great when you're drinking a Coke."

It takes a powerful campaign to deliver such a message. In the recent past, Coca-Cola has leaned on the services of an advertising agency: McCann-Erickson.

McCann-Erickson started out, Zyman said, with 36 lines. Chop them up. Juggle them around. Fool with them. Whittle them down to a little collection of thoughts.

Set them to music, 4-4 times, key of C. Not too many sharps at the beginning.

This song mentions smiles, spending time with family and friends, big taste. It gets fancy musically, too, with lots of major sevenths toward the end.

The song is a compendium of some of the best lines in Coke advertising history. It builds on the past. Reinforces.

"Maybe it's so basic that, the explanation will sound stupid," Zyman said, "but it's a soft drink. We think it is the best soft drink. It's the most refreshing soft drink. Coke is it!"

The next step, Zyman said, was to make the song into a campaign. The call went out for exciting things to marry visually to the new Coke slogan.

How does Grambling University's marching band sound for excitement? And the cheerleaders and some locals at a big bonfire at Rice University?

And a sweaty farmer out in the he fields, just busting his back from work and worry about commodities prices. Back home, his family is preparing a surprise party. Guess what they are going to drink?

From Los Angeles, school kids; blue collared workers huddled around a Coke machine during a break; some classy actors struggling through rehearsals in New York City. Tie it all together with the song. Segue to everyone drinking Coke.

What does putting those three little words in the ears of every American cost?

Zyman won't say, but the company bought time on each top-rated network TV show to launch the campaign. On one night alone, 90 million American consumers got the new word about Coke. If the slogan catches on, Zyman hopes to keep it for a decade. If not, maybe it wasn't the real thing after all.

Attachment 4

Peanut Butter Score Sheet

Scoring   **1 = Poor**   **2 = Fair**   **3 = Average**   **4 = Good**   **5 = Excellent**

Directions: You will test four brands of peanut butter in four categories. The categories are: taste, texture, spreadability, and the amount of additives. Read the instructions for testing that appear on the bottom of the worksheet. Then, test each brand and score it from 1 (poor) through 5 (excellent) in each category. Write the scores in the blanks provided.

Brand #1	**Brand #2**
Taste: _____	Taste: _____
Texture: _____	Texture: _____
Spreadability: _____	Spreadability: _____
Additives: _____	Additives: _____
Brand #3	**Brand #4**
Taste: _____	Taste: _____
Texture: _____	Texture: _____
Spreadability: _____	Spreadability: _____
Additives: _____	Additives: _____

Instructions for Testing:

1. **Taste**. Use a knife to scoop out a small amount of peanut butter and spread it on a cracker. Bite half of the cracker and chew it carefully. Is the peanut flavor of the butter strong? Is the peanut butter too sweet or not sweet enough? Is it too salty? Does it have an oily flavor? Give high scores to a peanut butter with a good flavor.

2. **Texture**. Bite off the other half of the cracker. Does the peanut butter stick to the roof of your mouth? Is it thick and greasy, or is it light and airy? Is it dry and crumbly, or is it moist? Is the peanut butter difficult to swallow? Give high scores to peanut butter with an easy-to-eat texture.

3. **Spreadability**: Does the peanut butter spread smoothly? Or, does it crumble? Look at the peanut butter closely. Does it have tiny specks or is it all the same color? Give high scores to the peanut butter that spreads easily, is smooth, and looks even in color.

4. **Additives**. Peanut butter is mostly ground peanuts and vegetable oil. Additives are the other items. They are added to perk up taste. Read the list of ingredients next to the jar of peanut butter. Peanut butter with a low amount of sugar, salt, sweeteners (such as dextrose or corn sweetener), and other additives should receive a high score. A lot of additives makes the peanut butter less healthful, or nutritious.

Attachment 5

Soda Competition

Evaluate each group's presentation on a scale from 1 (lowest) to 4 (highest) based on the four criteria.

	Billboard	Soda Can	Taste	Commercial	Total
1	1 2 3 4	1 2 3 4	1 2 3 4	1 2 3 4	
2	1 2 3 4	1 2 3 4	1 2 3 4	1 2 3 4	
3	1 2 3 4	1 2 3 4	1 2 3 4	1 2 3 4	
4	1 2 3 4	1 2 3 4	1 2 3 4	1 2 3 4	

Unit 13
Law: The Next Generation

Areas of Giftedness
- General Intellectual Ability
- Leadership
- Specific Academic Areas:
  - Creative Thinking
  - Fine Arts
  - Language Arts
  - Social Studies

Grade Levels
4–6

Duration
12 weeks

Generalizations
- Exploring historical legal benchmarks promotes understanding.
- Relationships exist between present and future laws of societies.
- Exploring human rights issues broadens understanding of ourselves and others.
- Experiencing authentic situations improves problem solving.
- Connections exist between conflict and the generation of laws.

**Theme:
Explorations**

**Grade Levels:
4–6**

**Developers:
Laura Young
and
Josette Honus**

Objective	Activities	Interdisciplinary Connections
• By investigating historic legal benchmarks, students will trace the development of present day laws to understand a society's need for a legal system.	• Uncover historical codes, characters, oaths, morals, and resolutions. (Discuss.) Show understanding of these studied benchmarks by role playing.	• Language Arts, Social Studies
	• Use Kohlberg's moral development theory to document personal responses to legal benchmarks.	• Language Arts, Social Studies, Psychology
	• Create a timeline to order various historical codes and benchmarks according to chronological occurrences.	• Language Arts, Social Studies
• Students will analyze current laws and evaluate specific Supreme Court decisions as they relate to U.S. Constitution.	• Investigate familiar civil and criminal court cases.
• Write dialogues for responding to the court's power and present to class.	• Social Studies, Language Arts
	• Recognize future criminal trends that may occur because of advances in science and technology. Create a class chart.	• Social Studies, Language Arts, Science
	• Discover current issues and problems of law by using periodicals. Create a collage to reflect such issues. Present to the class.	• Social Studies, Language Arts
	• Translate ideals into a personal code and create a written oath, code, or pledge.	• Social Studies, Language Arts
	• Interpret responses to selected legal benchmarks by using Kohlberg's theory of moral development. Create an evaluation grid.	• Language Arts, Social Studies
	• Dissect Bill of Rights and categorize the parts as civil or criminal. Display findings in a graphic organizer.	• Language Arts, Social Studies
	• Relate cases to types of crimes and use finds to create a matching game.
• Create "wanted" posters for criminal acts committed by characters in rhymes, fairy tales, or mythology.	• Language Arts, Social Studies
	• Organize a "point-counter-point" discussion about methods of formal punishment for criminal actions. Present to class.
• Compile a photo essay to display a variety of problems involving human rights.	• Social Studies
	• Add amendments to the constitution to make it more responsive to selected human rights issues.	• Social Studies, Fine Arts, Leadership

Authentic Methods and Context	Resources	Assessment
	• *Grolier's Encyclopedia,* CD-ROM.	
	• *Cobblestone* Magazine.	
		• Completed oath will be self-evaluated by student and teacher chosen on a reflection log.
	• Crowell, C.E. (1991). *You and the law.* Educational Design.	
• Work with members of high school debate team to learn debate techniques.		• Photo essay may be evaluated by a teacher using selected criteria by teacher on a rating scale. Public forum presentation evaluated by teacher and student-created rubric.

Objective	Activities	Interdisciplinary Connections
• In their study of human rights issues, students will model a formal debate on an issue regarding media and the law, medical laws, or corporal punishment and will share ideas through a video-taped commentary. See Lesson Plan 1, Page 124	• **Justify a position on an issue regarding media and the law, medical laws, or human rights. Conduct a formal debate and share results through a videotaped commentary.**	• Language Arts, Social Studies, Fine Arts
	• **Dramatize or create a puppet show using conflict resolution to remedy conflicts presented in fairy tales.**	• Language Arts, Social Studies
	• **Compare and contrast different degrees of conflict using periodicals describing local, national, and international conflicts. Make a Venn diagram to display findings.**	• Language Arts, Social Studies
• In their study of human rights issues, students will amend the U.S. Constitution to meet the future needs of a society through a Continental Congress and share ideas through a dramatization. See Lesson Plan 2, Page 124	• **Create a dramatization in which the U.S. Constitution is amended to meet the future needs of a society through a mock-Continental Congress.**	• Language Arts, Social Studies, Fine Arts
	• **Solve a conflict scenario using legal means through a mock-trial.**	• Language Arts, Social Studies, Fine Arts
	• **Predict how today's society would perceive the crimes committed by nursery rhyme or fairy tale characters. Share ideas in a rap or a poem.**	• Language Arts
	• **Design criteria for sentencing alleged fairy tale or nursery rhyme criminals. Display criteria in a grid.**	• Language Arts, Social Studies
	• **Construct a new moral code for the class of 2020.**	• Language Arts, Social Studies
	• **Declare a civic, civil, and criminal code from the moral code of 2020 on an evaluation grid.**	• Language Arts, Social Studies
• The students will predict future problems and ramifications of existing laws that may occur due to advances in science and technology to develop appropriate legislative changes.	• **Predict necessary laws for the future due to science and technological advances. Create a news broadcast or mock-interview with a legislator.**	• Science, Technology
	• **Create an editorial essay explaining legal problems relating to medical issues such as: cloning, gene manipulation, cryonics, transplants, and euthanasia.**	• Language Arts, Social Studies

Authentic Methods and Context	Resources	Assessment
	• Riekes, L. (1980). *Courts and trials.* St. Paul, MN: West Publishing Company. • Riekes, L. (1980). *Lawmaking.* St. Paul, MN: West Publishing Company.	• Teacher and student developed evaluation instrument will be used for teacher and self-performance assessment.
• Students participate in local decision making program such as teen court.		
• Create a program to be used with juveniles to address prevention of crime and abiding by the law. Propose and defend its use to local juvenile and school officials.	• Miller, M. (1992). *You be the jury.* Apple.	

Lesson Plan 1

Law: The Next Generation
Measurement Skills

Lesson Objectives
In their study of human rights issues, students will model a formal debate on an issue regarding media and the law, medical laws, and will share their ideas through a videotaped commentary.

Prerequisite Skills
Debate skills, knowledge of human rights issues.

Materials
General classroom supplies, camcorder and tripod, sample video of a taped commentary.

Introduction
Review human rights issues by webbing current topics on the board.

Activity Description
1. Introduce videotaped sample commentary of a high school debate team by asking how to design a high quality commentary and videotape. Set and describe criteria as a class.
2. Develop with students desired outcomes and rating methods for a high quality videotaped commentary on a rating rubric.
3. Support small groups of students as they create videotaped commentaries on a modeled human rights issue debate.

Closure
Summarize a formal debate on a human rights issue by asking students to share their commentaries and decide whether the issues were adequately addressed.

Extensions
Share ideas on human rights issues by composing a letter to the editor.

Assessment
Class created rating rubric will be used to evaluate the videotaped commentary.

Lesson Plan 2

Law: The Next Generation
Amending the Constitution

Lesson Objectives
In their study of human rights issues, students will amend the U.S. Constitution to meet the future needs of a society through a Continental Congress and share their ideas through a dramatization.

Prerequisite Skills
Knowledge of legal benchmarks, civil-criminal law (now and in the future), human rights issues, how conflicts generate law.

Materials
U.S. Constitution, costumes, video camera (optional), *Bloom's Taxonomy Chart*, overhead projector and transparency.

Introduction
View a short video clip of a Continental Congress reenactment and a short clip of a present-day legislative session. Compare and contrast, establish purposes of each.

Activity Description
1. Review U.S. Constitution by discussing elements of the Constitution.
2. Review synthesis evaluation level by referring to *Bloom's Taxonomy Chart*.
3. Discuss desired outcomes of the Continental Congress dramatization and record main points on an overhead transparency.
4. Assist the group to choose a president, recorder, and tie-breaker. Organize discussion groups to represent various geographical areas and concerns in a simulated Continental Congress. Facilitate presentation of proposed amendments in a public forum.
5. Finalize the chosen amendments by guiding classroom discussion.

Closure
Share and critique chosen amendments.

Extensions
    Compile a list of chosen amendments and send to a Supreme Court Justice requesting input and ideas.

Assessment
    Public forum presentations will be evaluated by teacher and student-created rubric.